Linked Lexical Knowledge Bases

Foundations and Applications

Synthesis Lectures on Human Language Technologies

Editor
Graeme Hirst, *University of Toronto*

Synthesis Lectures on Human Language Technologies is edited by Graeme Hirst of the University of Toronto. The series consists of 50- to 150-page monographs on topics relating to natural language processing, computational linguistics, information retrieval, and spoken language understanding. Emphasis is on important new techniques, on new applications, and on topics that combine two or more HLT subfields.

Linked Lexical Knowledge Bases: Foundations and Applications

Iryna Gurevych, Judith Eckle-Kohler, and Michael Matuschek

ISBN: 978-3-031-01034-7   paperback
ISBN: 978-3-031-02162-6   ebook

DOI 10.1007/978-3-031-02162-6

A Publication in the Springer series
SYNTHESIS LECTURES ON HUMAN LANGUAGE TECHNOLOGIES

Lecture #34
Series Editor: Graeme Hirst, *University of Toronto*
Series ISSN
Print 1947-4040   Electronic 1947-4059

Linked Lexical Knowledge Bases

Foundations and Applications

Iryna Gurevych, Judith Eckle-Kohler, and Michael Matuschek
Technische Universität Darmstadt, Germany

SYNTHESIS LECTURES ON HUMAN LANGUAGE TECHNOLOGIES #34

ABSTRACT

This book conveys the fundamentals of Linked Lexical Knowledge Bases (LLKB) and sheds light on their different aspects from various perspectives, focusing on their construction and use in natural language processing (NLP). It characterizes a wide range of both expert-based and collaboratively constructed lexical knowledge bases. Only basic familiarity with NLP is required and this book has been written for both students and researchers in NLP and related fields who are interested in knowledge-based approaches to language analysis and their applications.

Lexical Knowledge Bases (LKBs) are indispensable in many areas of natural language processing, as they encode human knowledge of language in machine readable form, and as such, they are required as a reference when machines attempt to interpret natural language in accordance with human perception. In recent years, numerous research efforts have led to the insight that to make the best use of available knowledge, the orchestrated exploitation of different LKBs is necessary. This allows us to not only extend the range of covered words and senses, but also gives us the opportunity to obtain a richer knowledge representation when a particular meaning of a word is covered in more than one resource. Examples where such an orchestrated usage of LKBs proved beneficial include word sense disambiguation, semantic role labeling, semantic parsing, and text classification.

This book presents different kinds of automatic, manual, and collaborative linkings between LKBs. A special chapter is devoted to the linking algorithms employing text-based, graph-based, and joint modeling methods. Following this, it presents a set of higher-level NLP tasks and algorithms, effectively utilizing the knowledge in LLKBs. Among them, you will find advanced methods, e.g., distant supervision, or continuous vector space models of knowledge bases (KB), that have become widely used at the time of this book's writing. Finally, multilingual applications of LLKB's, such as cross-lingual semantic relatedness and computer-aided translation are discussed, as well as tools and interfaces for exploring LLKBs, followed by conclusions and future research directions.

KEYWORDS

lexical knowledge bases, linked lexical knowledge bases, sense alignment, word sense disambiguation, graph-based methods, text similarity, distant supervision, automatic knowledge base construction, continuous vector space models, multilingual applications

Contents

Foreword

Lexical semantic knowledge is vital for most tasks in natural language processing (NLP). Such knowledge has been captured through two main approaches. The first is the *knowledge-based* approach, in which human linguistic knowledge is encoded directly in a structured form, resulting in various types of lexical knowledge bases. The second is the *corpus-based* approach, in which lexical semantic knowledge is learned from corpora and then represented in either explicit or implicit manners.

Historically, the knowledge-based approach preceded the corpus-based one, while the latter has been dominating the center-stage of NLP research in the last decades. Yet, the development and use of lexical knowledge bases (LKBs) continued to be a major thread. An illustration of this fact may be found in the number of citations for the fundamental 1998 WordNet book [Fellbaum, 1998a], over 12,000 at the time of writing (according to Google Scholar), which somewhat exceeds the number of citations for the primary text book on statistical NLP from about the same period [Manning and Schütze, 1999]. Despite the overwhelming success of corpus-based methods, whether supervised or unsupervised, their output may be quite noisy, particularly when it comes to modeling fine-grained lexical knowledge such as distinct word senses or concrete lexical semantic relationships. Human encoding, on the other hand, provides more precise knowledge at the fine-grained level. The ongoing popular use of LKBs, and particularly of WordNet, seems to indicate that they still provide substantial complementary information relative to corpus-based methods (see Shwartz et al. [2015] for a concrete evaluation showing the complementary behavior of corpus-based word embeddings and information from multiple LKBs).

While WordNet has been by far the most widely-used lexical resource, it does not provide the full spectrum of needed lexical knowledge, which brings us to the theme of the current book. As reviewed in Chapter 2, additional lexical information has been encoded in quite a few LKBs, either by experts or by web communities through collaborative efforts. In particular, collaborative resources provide the opportunity to obtain much larger and more frequently updated resources than is possible with expert work. Knowledge resources like Wikipedia[1] or Wikidata[2] include vast lexical information about individual entities and domain specific terminology across many domains, which falls beyond the scope of WordNet. Hence, it would be ideal for NLP technology to utilize in an integrated manner the union of information available in a multitude of lexical resources. As an illustrating example, consider an application setting, like a question answering scenario, which requires knowing that Deep Purple was a group of people. We may

---

[1]https://www.wikipedia.org
[2]https://www.wikidata.org

find in Wikipedia that it was a "band," map this term to its right sense in WordNet and then follow a hypernymy chain to "organization," whose definition includes "a group of people."

As hinted in the above example, to allow such resource integration we need effective methods for linking, or aligning, the word senses or concepts encoded in various resources. Accordingly, the main technical focus of this book is about existing resource integration efforts, resource linking algorithms, and the utility of such algorithms within disambiguation tasks. Hence, this book would first be of high value for researchers interested in creating or linking LKBs, as well as for developers of NLP algorithms and applications who would like to leverage linked lexical resources. An important aspect is the development and use of linked lexical resources in multiple languages, addressed in Chapter 7.

Looking forward, maybe the most interesting research prospect for linked lexical knowledge bases is their integration with corpus-based machine learning approaches. A relatively simple form of combining the information in LKBs with corpus-based information is to use the former, via distant supervision, to create training data for the latter (discussed in Section 6.2). A more fundamental research direction is to create a unified knowledge representation framework, which integrates directly the human-encoded information in LKBs with information obtained by corpus-based methods. A promising framework for such integrated representation has emerged recently, under the "embedding" paradigm, where dense continuous vectors are used to represent linguistic objects, as reviewed in Section 6.3. Such representations, i.e., embeddings, have been initially created separately from corpus data—based on corpus co-occurrences, as well as from knowledge bases—based on and leveraging their rich internal structure. Further research suggested methods for creating unified representations, based on hybrid objective functions that consider both corpus and knowledge base structure. While this research line is still in initial phases, it has the potential to truly integrate corpus-based and human-encoded knowledge, and thus unify these two research endeavors which have been pursued mostly separately in the past. From this perspective, and assuming that human-encoded lexical knowledge can provide useful additional information on top of corpus-based information, the current book should be useful for any researcher who aims to advance state of the art in lexical semantics.

While considering the integration of implicit corpus-based and explicit human-encoded information, we may notice that the joint embedding approach goes the "implicit way." While joint embeddings do encode information coming from both types of resources, this information is encoded in opaque continuous vectors, which are not immediately interpretable, thus losing the transparency of the original symbolically-encoded human knowledge. Indeed, developing methods for interpreting embedding-based representations is an actively pursued theme, but it is yet to be seen whether such attempts will succeed to preserve the interpretability of LKB information. Alternatively, one might imagine developing integrated corpus-based and knowledge-based representations that would inherently involve explicit symbolic representations, even though, currently, this might be seen as wishful thinking.

Finally, one would hope that the current book, and work on new lexical representations in general, would encourage researchers to better connect the development of knowledge resources with generic aspects of their utility for NLP tasks. Consider for example the common use of the lexical semantic relationships in WordNet for lexical inference. Typically, WordNet relations are utilized in an application to infer the meaning of one word from another in order to bridge lexical gaps, such as when different words are used in a question and in an answer passage. While this type of inference has been applied in numerous works, surprisingly there are no well-defined methods that indicate how to optimally exploit WordNet for lexical inference. Instead, each work applies its own heuristics, with respect to the types of WordNet links that should be followed, the length of link chains, the senses to be considered, etc. In this state of affairs, it is hard for LKB developers to assess which components of the knowledge and representations that they create are truly useful. Similar challenges are faced when trying to assess the utility of vector-based representations.[3]

Eventually, one might expect that generic methods for utilizing and assessing lexical knowledge representations would guide their development and reveal their optimal form, based on either implicit or explicit representations, or both.

Ido Dagan
Department of Computer Science
Bar-Ilan University, Israel

---

[3]One effort to address these challenges is the ACL 2016 workshop on Evaluating Vector Space Representations for NLP, whose mission statement is "To develop new and improved ways of measuring the quality or understanding the properties of vector-space representations in NLP." https://sites.google.com/site/repevalacl16/.

Preface

MOTIVATION

Lexical Knowledge Bases (LKBs) are indispensable in many areas of natural language processing (NLP). They strive to encode the human knowledge of language in machine-readable form, and as such they are required as a reference when machines are supposed to interpret natural language in accordance with the human perception. Examples for such tasks are word sense disambiguation (WSD) and information retrieval (IR). The aim of WSD is to determine the correct meaning of ambiguous words in context, and in order to formalize this task, a so-called sense inventory is required, i.e., a resource encoding the different meanings a word can express. In IR, the goal is to retrieve, given a user query formulating a specific information need, the documents from a collection which fulfill this need best. Here, knowledge is also necessary to correctly interpret short and often ambiguous queries, and to relate them to the set of documents.

Nowadays, LKBs exist in many variations. For instance, the META-SHARE repository[4] lists over 1,000 different lexical resources, and the LRE Map[5] contains more than 3,900 resources which have been proposed as a knowledge source for natural language processing systems. A main distinction, which is also made in this book, is between expert-built and collaboratively constructed resources. While the distinction is not always clean-cut, the former are generally resources which are created by a limited set of expert editors or professionals using their personal introspection, corpus evidence, or other means to obtain the knowledge. Collaboratively constructed resources, on the other hand, are open for every volunteer to edit, with no or only few restrictions such as registration for a website. Intuitively, the quality of the entries should be lower when laypeople are involved in the creation of a resource, but it has been shown that the collaborative process of correcting errors and extending articles (also known as the "wisdom of the crowds"; Surowiecki [2005]) can lead to results of remarkable quality [Giles, 2005]. The most prominent example is Wikipedia, the largest encyclopedia and one of the largest knowledge sources known. Although originally not meant for that purpose, it has also become a major source of knowledge for all kinds of NLP applications, many of which we will discuss in this book [Medelyan et al., 2009].

Apart from the basic distinction with regard to the production process, LKBs exist in many flavors. Some are focusing on encyclopedic knowledge (Wikipedia), others resemble language dictionaries (Wiktionary) or aim to describe the concepts used in human language and the re-

---

[4]http://www.meta-share.eu
[5]http://www.resourcebook.eu

lationships between them from a psycholinguistic (Princeton WordNet [Fellbaum, 1998a]) or a semantic (FrameNet [Ruppenhofer et al., 2010]) perspective. Another important distinction is between monolingual resources, i.e., those covering only one language, and multilingual ones, which not only feature entries in different languages but usually also provide translations. However, despite the large number of existing LKBs, the growing demand for large-scale LKBs in different languages is still not met. While Princeton WordNet has emerged as a de facto standard for English NLP, for most languages corresponding resources are either considerably smaller or missing altogether. For instance, the *Open Multilingual Wordnet* project lists only 25 wordnets in languages other than English, and only few of them (like the Finnish or Polish versions) match or surpass Princeton WordNet's size [Bond and Foster, 2013]. Multilingual efforts such as Wiktionary or OmegaWiki provide a viable option for such cases and seem especially suitable for smaller languages due to their open construction paradigm and low entry requirements [Matuschek et al., 2013], but there are still considerable gaps in coverage which the corresponding language communities are struggling to fill.

A closely related problem is that, even if comprehensive resources are available for a specific language, there usually does not exist a single resource which works best for all application scenarios or purposes, as different LKBs cover not only different words and senses, but sometimes even completely different information types. For instance, the knowledge about verb classes (i.e., groups of verbs which share certain properties) contained in VerbNet is not covered by WordNet, although it might be useful depending on the task, for example to provide subcategorization information when parsing low frequency verbs.

These considerations have led to the insight that, to make the best possible use of the available knowledge, the orchestrated exploitation of different LKBs is necessary. This lets us not only extend the range of covered words and senses, but more importantly, gives us the opportunity to obtain a richer knowledge representation when a particular meaning of a word is covered in more than one resource.

Examples where such a joint usage of LKBs proved beneficial include WSD using aligned WordNet and Wikipedia in BabelNet [Navigli and Ponzetto, 2012a], semantic role labeling (SRL) using a mapping between PropBank, VerbNet and FrameNet [Palmer, 2009], and the construction of a semantic parser using a combination of FrameNet, WordNet, and VerbNet [Shi and Mihalcea, 2005]. These combined resources, known as *Linked Lexical Knowledge Bases* (LLKB), are the focus of this book, and we shed light on their different aspects from various angles.

TARGET AUDIENCE AND FOCUS

This book is intended to convey a fundamental understanding of Linked Lexical Knowledge Bases, in particular their construction and use, in the context of NLP. Our target audience are students and researchers from NLP and related fields who are interested in knowledge-based approaches. We assume only basic familiarity with NLP methods and thus this book can be used both for self-study and for teaching at an introductory level.

Note that the focus of this book is mostly on sense linking between general-purpose LKBs, which are most commonly used in NLP. While we acknowledge that there are many efforts of linking LKBs, for instance, to ontologies or domain-specific resources, we only discuss them briefly where appropriate and provide references for readers interested in these more specific linking scenarios. The same is true for the recent efforts in creating ontologies from LKBs and formalizing the relationships between them—while we give an introduction to this topic in Section 1.3, we realize that this diverse area of research deserves a book of its own, which indeed has been published recently [Chiarcos et al., 2012]. Our attention is rather on the actual algorithmic linking process, and the benefits it brings for applications. Furthermore, we put an emphasis on monolingual linking efforts (i.e., between resources in the same language), as the vast majority of algorithms have covered this scenario in the past and cross-lingual approaches were mostly direct derivatives thereof, for instance by introducing machine translation as an intermediate component (cf. Chapter 3). Nevertheless, we recognize the increasing importance of multilingual NLP and thus provide a dedicated chapter covering applications in this area (Chapter 6).

OUTLINE

After providing a brief description of the typographic conventions which we applied throughout this book, we start by introducing and comparatively analyzing a selection of LKBs which have been widely used in NLP (Chapter 1). Our description of these LKBs provides a foundation for the main part of this book, where their integration into LLKBs is considered from various different angles. We include expert-built LKBs, such as WordNet, as well as collaboratively constructed resources, such as Wikipedia and Wiktionary, and also cover established standards and representation formats which are relevant in this context.

Then, in Chapter 2, we give a more formal definition of LLKBs, and also of word sense linking, which is crucial for combining different resources semantically, and thus is of utmost importance. We go on by describing various LLKBs which have been suggested, putting a focus on current large-scale projects which dominate the field, but also considering smaller, more specialized initiatives which have yielded important insights and paved the way for large-scale resource integration.

In Chapter 3, we approach the core issue of automatic word sense linking. While the notion of similar or even equivalent word senses in different resources is intuitively understandable and often (but now always) quite easily grasped by humans, it poses a complex challenge for automatic processing due to word ambiguities, different sense granularities and information types [Navigli, 2006]. First, to contextualize the challenge, we describe some related tasks in NLP and other fields, and outline how word sense linking relates to them. Then, we discuss in detail different ways to automatically create sense links between LKBs, based on textual descriptions of senses (i.e., glosses), the structure of the resources, or a combination thereof. The broader context of

LLKBs lies of course not in the mere linking of resources for its own sake, but in the potential it holds for NLP applications.

Thus, in the following chapters, we present a selection of methods and applications where the use of LLKBs leads to particular benefits for NLP. In Chapter 4, we describe how the disambiguation of textual units benefits from the richer structure and combined knowledge, and also how the clustering of fine-grained word senses by exploiting 1:n links improves WSD accuracy. Building on that, we present more advanced disambiguation techniques in Chapter 5, including a discussion of using LLKBs for distant supervision and in neural vector space models, which are two recent and especially promising topics in machine learning for NLP. In Chapter 6 we briefly present multilingual applications, and computer-aided translation in particular, and show how they benefit from linked multilingual resources. Finally, in Chapter 7, we supplement our considerations of LLKB applications by discussing the enabling technologies, i.e., how LLKBs can be accessed via user interfaces and application programming interfaces. Based on the discussion of access paths for single resources, we describe how interfaces for current complex linked resources have evolved to cater to the needs of researchers and end users.

Chapter 8 concludes this book and points out directions for future work.

TYPOGRAPHIC CONVENTIONS

- Newly introduced terms and example lemmas are typed in *italics*.

- Synsets (groups of synonymous words) are enclosed by curly brackets, e.g., {*car, automobile*}.

- Concepts are typed in small caps, e.g., STREET VEHICLE WITH FOUR WHEELS.

- Relations between senses are written as pairs in parentheses, e.g., *(car, vehicle)*.

- Classes of the *Lexical Markup Framework* (LMF) standard are printed in a monospace font starting with an upper case letter (e.g., `LexicalEntry`).

- LMF data categories are printed in a monospace font starting with a lower case letter (e.g., `partOfSpeech`).

We acknowledge support by the Volkswagen Foundation as part of the Lichtenberg-Professorship Program under grant No. I/82806, by the German Institute for Educational Research (DIPF), and by the German Research Foundation under grant No. GU 798/17-1. We also thank our colleagues and students for their contributions to this book.

Iryna Gurevych, Judith Eckle-Kohler, and Michael Matuschek
July 2016

Acknowledgments

…Mentors matter! The authors of the book are very grateful to each and everyone who generously offered their guidance, support, advice, strategic feedback and valuable insights of all kinds during our professional careers. This helped us grow, learn, identify and accomplish the right goals, including this very book.

Iryna Gurevych, Judith Eckle-Kohler, and Michael Matuschek
July 2016

CHAPTER 1

Lexical Knowledge Bases

In this chapter we give an overview of different types of lexical knowledge bases that are used in natural language processing (NLP). We cover widely known expert-built Lexical Knowledge Bases (LKBs), and also collaborative LKBs, i.e., those created by a large community of layman collaborators. First we define our terminology, then we give a broad overview of various kinds of LKBs that play an important role in NLP. For particular resource-specific details, we refer the reader to the respective reference publications.

Definition <u>Lexical Knowledge Base:</u> Lexical knowledge bases (LKBs) are digital knowledge bases that provide lexical information on words (including multi-word expressions) of a particular language.[1] By word, we mean word form, or more specifically, the canonical base word form which is called *lemma*. For example, *write* is the lemma of *wrote*. Most LKBs provide lexical information for lemmas. A *lexeme* is a word in combination with a part of speech (POS), such as noun, verb or adjective. The majority of LKBs specify the part of speech of the lemmas listed, i.e., provide lexical information on lexemes.

The pairings of lemma and meaning are called word senses or just *senses*. We use the terms *meaning* and *concept* synonymously in this book to refer to the possibly language-independent part of a sense. Each sense is typically identified by a unique sense identifier. For example, there are two meanings of the verb *write* which give rise to two different senses:[2] (*write*, "to communicate with someone in writing") and (*write*, "to produce a literary work"). Accordingly, a LKB might use identifiers, such as `write01` and `write02` to distinguish between the former and the latter sense. The set of all senses listed in a LKB is called its *sense inventory*.

Depending on their particular focus, LKBs can contain a variety of lexical information, including morphological, phonetic, syntactic, semantic, and pragmatic information. This book focuses on LKBs that provide lexical information on the word sense level, i.e., information that is sensitive to the meaning of a word and is therefore attached to a pairing of lemma and meaning rather than to the lemma itself. Not included in our definition are LKBs that only provide morphological information about the inflectional and derivational properties of words.

The following list provides an overview of the main lexical information types distinguished at the level of word senses.

---

[1]It is important to note that LKBs provide lexical information on word types rather than word tokens.
[2]It should be noted that in our example, the meaning is defined in natural language. Alternatively, the meaning of a word can be defined more formally using, e.g., first-order logic.

- **Sense definition**—A definition of the sense in natural language (also called gloss) meant for human interpretation; for example, "to communicate with someone in writing" is a sense definition for the sense `write01` given above.

- **Sense examples**—Example sentences which illustrate the sense in context; for example, *He wrote her an email.* is a sense example of the sense `write01`.

- **Sense relations**—Lexical-semantic relations to other senses. We list the most salient ones.

  – *Synonymy* connects senses which are lexically different but share the same meaning. Synonymy is reflexive, symmetrical, and transitive. For example, the verbs *change* and *modify* are synonyms[3] as they share the meaning "cause to change."

    Some resources such as WordNet subsume synonymous senses into *synsets*. However, for the linking algorithms presented in this book, we will usually not distinguish between *sense* and *synset*, as for most discussions and experiments in this particular context they can be used interchangeably.

  – *Antonymy* is a relation in which the source and target sense have opposite meanings (e.g., *tall* and *small*).

  – *Hyponymy* denotes a semantic relation where the target sense has a more specific meaning than the source sense (e.g., from *limb* to *arm*).

  – *Hypernymy* is the inverse relation of hyponymy and thus denotes a semantic relation in which the target sense has a more general meaning than the source sense.

- **Syntactic behavior**—Lexical-syntactic properties, such as the valency of verbs, i.e., the number and type of syntactic arguments a verb takes; for example, the verb *change* ("cause to change") can take a noun phrase subject and a noun phrase object as syntactic arguments, as in: *She*[subject] *changed the rules*[object].

  In LKBs, valency is represented by subcategorization frames (short: subcat frames). They specify syntactic arguments of verbs, but also of other predicate-like lexemes that can take syntactic arguments, e.g., nouns able to take a that-clause (*announcement, fact*) or adjectives taking a prepositional argument (*proud of, happy about*). For syntactic arguments, subcat frames typically specify the *syntactic category* (e.g., noun phrase, verb phrase) and *grammatical function* (e.g., subject, object).

- **Predicate argument structure information**—For predicate-like words, such as verbs, this refers to a definition of the *semantic predicate* and information on the semantic arguments, including:

  – *their semantic role* according to an inventory of semantic roles given in the context of a particular linguistic theory. There is no standard inventory of semantic roles, i.e., there

---

[3]For brevity, we might use lemmas to denote senses.

are linguistic theories assuming small sets of about 40 roles, and others specifying very large sets of several hundred roles. Examples of typical semantic roles are *Agent* or *Patient*; and

- *selectional preference information*, which specifies the preferred semantic category of an argument, e.g., whether it is a *human* or an *artifact*.

   For example, the sense *change* ("cause to change") corresponds to a semantic predicate which can be described in natural language as "an Agent causes an Entity to change;" Agent and Entity are semantic roles of this predicate: *She*[Agent] *changed the rules*[Entity]; the preferred semantic category of *Agent* is *human*.

- **Related forms**—Word forms that are *morphologically* related, such as compounds or verbs derived from nouns; for example, the verb *buy* ("purchase") is derivationally related to the noun *buy*, while on the other hand *buy* ("accept as true" e.g., *I can't buy this story*) is not derivationally related to the noun *buy*.

- **Equivalents**—Translations of the sense in other languages; for example, *kaufen* is the German translation of *buy* ("purchase"), while *abkaufen* is the German translation of *buy* ("accept as true")

- **Sense links**—Mappings of senses to equivalent senses in other LKBs; for example, the sense *change* (*Cause_change*) in FrameNet can be linked to the equivalent sense *change* ("cause to change") in WordNet.

There are different ways to organize a LKB, for example, by grouping synonymous senses, or by grouping senses with the same lemma. The latter organization is the traditional head-word based organization used in dictionaries [Atkins and Rundell, 2008] where a LKB consists of lexical entries which group senses under a common headword (the lemma).

There is a large number of so-called Machine-readable Dictionaries (MRD), mostly digitized versions of traditional print dictionaries [Lew, 2011, Soanes and Stevenson, 2003], but also some MRDs are only available in digitized form, such as DANTE [Kilgarriff, 2010] or DWDS[4] for German [Klein and Geyken, 2010]. We will not include them in our overview for the following reasons: MRDs have traditionally been built by lexicographers and are targeted toward human use, rather than toward use by automatic processing components in NLP. While MRDs provide information useful in NLP, such as sense definitions, sense examples, as well as grammatical information (e.g., about syntactic behavior), the representation of this information in MRDs usually lacks a strict, formal structure, and thus the information usually suffers from ambiguities. Although such ambiguities can easily be resolved by humans, they are a source of noise when the dictionary entries are processed fully automatically.

Our definition of LKBs also covers domain-specific terminology resources (e.g., the *Unified Medical Language System* (UMLS) metathesaurus of medical terms [Bodenreider, 2004]) that

---

[4]www.dwds.de

provide domain-specific terms and sense relations between them. However, we do not include these domain-specific resources in our overview, because we used general language LKBs to develop and evaluate the linking algorithms presented in Chapter 3.

1.1   EXPERT-BUILT LEXICAL KNOWLEDGE BASES

Expert-built LKBs, in our definition of this term, are resources which are designed, created and edited by a group of designated experts, e.g., (computational) lexicographers, (computational) linguists, or psycho-linguists. While it is possible that there is influence on the editorial process from the outside (e.g., via suggestions provided by users or readers), there is usually no direct means of public participation. This form of resource creation has been predominant since the earliest days of lexicography (or, more broadly, creation of language resources), and while the reliance on expert knowledge produces high quality resources, an obvious disadvantage are the slow production cycles—for all of the resources discussed in this section, it usually takes months (if not years) until a new version is published, while at the same time most of the information remains unchanged. This is due to the extensive effort needed for the creation of a resource of considerable size, in most cases provided by a very small group of people. Nevertheless, these resources play a major role in NLP. One reason is that up until recent years there were no real alternatives available, and some of these LKBs also cover aspects of language which are rather specific and not easily accessible for layman editors. We will present the most pertinent examples in this section.

1.1.1   WORDNETS

Wordnets define senses primarily by their relations to other senses, most notably the synonymy relation that is used to group synonymous senses into so-called synsets. Accordingly, synsets are the main organizational units in wordnets. In addition to synonymy, wordnets provide a large variety of additional sense relations. Most of the sense relations are defined on the synset level, i.e., between synsets, such as hypernymy or meronymy. Other sense relations, such as antonymy, are defined between individual senses, rather than between synsets. For example, while *evil* and *unworthy* are synonymous ("morally reprehensible" according to WordNet), their antonyms are different; *good* is the antonym of *evil* and *worthy* is the antonym of *unworthy*.

The Princeton WordNet for English [Fellbaum, 1998a] was the first such wordnet. It became the most popular wordnet and the most widely used LKB today. The creation of the Princeton WordNet is psycholinguisticially motivated, i.e., it aims to represent real-world concepts and relations between them as they are commonly perceived. Version 3.0 contains 117,659 synsets. Apart from its richness in sense relations, WordNet also contains coarse information about the syntactic behavior of verbs in the form of sentence frames (e.g., Somebody −$_s$ something).

There are various works based on the Princeton WordNet, such as the eXtended Word-Net [Mihalcea and Moldovan, 2001a], where all open class words in the sense definitions have been annotated with their WordNet sense to capture further relations between senses, WordNet

Domains [Bentivogli et al., 2004] which includes domain labels for senses, or SentiWordNet [Baccianella et al., 2010] which assigns sentiment scores to each synset of WordNet.

Wordnets in Other Languages   The Princeton WordNet for English inspired the creation of wordnets in many other languages worldwide and many of them also provide a linking of their senses to the Princeton WordNet. Examples include the Italian wordnet [Toral et al., 2010a], the Japanese wordnet [Isahara et al.], or the German wordnet GermaNet [Hamp and Feldweg, 1997].[5]

Often, wordnets in other languages have particular characteristics that distinguish them from the Princeton WordNet. GermaNet, for example, containing around 70,000 synsets in version 7.0, originally contained very few sense definitions, but unlike most other wordnets, provides detailed information on the syntactic behavior of verbs. For each verb sense, it lists possible subcat frames, distinguishing more than 200 different types.

It is important to point out, however, that in general, the Princeton WordNet provides richer information than the other wordnets. For example, it includes not only derivational morphological information, but also inflectional morphology analysis within its associated tools. It also provides an ordering of the senses based on the frequency information from the sense-annotated SemCor corpus—which is very useful for word sense disambiguation as many systems using WordNet rely on the sense ordering; see also examples in Chapter 4.

Information Types   The lexical information types prevailing in wordnets can be summarized as follows.

- **Sense definition**—Wordnets provide sense definitions at the synset level, i.e., all senses in a synset share the same sense definition.

- **Sense examples**—These are provided for individual senses.

- **Sense relations**—Most sense relations in wordnets are given at the synset level, i.e., all senses in a synset participate in such a relation.

  – A special case in wordnets is synonymy, because it is represented via synsets, rather than via relations between senses.

  – Most other sense relations are given on the synset level, e.g., hyponymy.

  – Few sense relations are defined between senses, e.g., antonymy, which does not always generalize to all members of a synset.

- **Syntactic behavior**—The degree of detail regarding the syntactic behavior varies from wordnet to wordnet. While the Princeton WordNet only distinguishes between few subcat frames, the German wordnet GermaNet distinguishes between about 200 very detailed subcat frames.

---

[5]A comprehensive overview is provided by the global wordnet association under `http://globalwordnet.org/wordnets-in-the-world/`.

- **Related forms**—The Princeton WordNet is rich in information about senses that are related via morphological derivation. Not all wordnets provide this information type.

1.1.2   FRAMENETS

LKBs modeled according to the theory of frame semantics [Fillmore, 1982] focus on word senses that evoke certain scenes or situations, so-called frames which are schematic representations of these. For instance, the "Killing" frame specifies a scene where "A Killer or Cause causes the death of the Victim." It can be evoked by verbs such as *assassinate, behead, terminate* or nouns such as *liquidation* or *massacre*.

The participants of these scenes (e.g., "Killer" and "Victim" in the "Killing" frame example), as well as other important elements (e.g., "Instrument" as "The device used by the Killer to bring about the death of the Victim" or "Place" as "The location where the death took place") constitute the semantic roles of the frame (called frame elements in frame semantics), and are typically realized in a sentence along with the frame-evoking element, as in: *Someone*[Killer] *tried to KILL him*[Victim] *with a parcel bomb*[Instrument].

The inventory of semantic roles used in FrameNet is very large and subject to further extension as FrameNet grows. Many semantic roles have frame-specific names, such as the "Killer" semantic role defined in the "Killing" frame.

Frames are the main organizational unit in framenets: they contain senses (represented by their lemma) that evoke the same frame. The majority of the frame-evoking words are verbs and other predicate-like lexemes: they can naturally be represented by frames, since predicates take arguments which can be characterized both syntactically (e.g., subject, direct object) and semantically via their semantic role.

There are semantic relations between frames (e.g., the "Is_Causative_of" relation between "Killing" and "Death" or the "Precedes" relation between "Being_born" and "Death" or "Dying"), and also between frame elements.

The English FrameNet [Baker et al., 1998, Ruppenhofer et al., 2010] was the first frame-semantic LKB and it is the most well-known one. Version 1.6 of FrameNet contains 1,205 frames. In FrameNet, senses are called lexical units. FrameNet does not provide explicit information about the syntactic behavior of word senses. However, the sense examples are annotated with syntactic information (FrameNet annotation sets) and from these annotations, subcat frames can be induced.

FrameNet is particularly rich in sense examples, which are selected based on lexicographic criteria, i.e., the sense examples are chosen to illustrate typical syntactic realizations of the frame elements. The sense examples are enriched with annotations of the frame and its elements, and thus provide information about the relative frequencies of the syntactic realizations of a particular frame element. For example, for the verb *kill*, a noun phrase with the grammatical function object is the most frequently used syntactic realization of the "Victim" role.

Framenets in Other Languages   The English FrameNet has spawned the construction of framenets in multiple other languages. For example, there are framenets for Spanish[6] [Subirats and Sato, 2004], Swedish[7] [Friberg Heppin and Toporowska Gronostaj, 2012], and Japanese[8] [Ohara, 2012]. For Danish, there is an ongoing effort to build a framenet based on a large-scale valency LKB that is manually being extended by frame-semantic information [Bick, 2011]. For German, there is a corpus annotated with FrameNet frames called SALSA [Burchardt et al., 2006].

Information Types   The following information types in the English FrameNet are most salient.

- **Sense definition**—For individual senses, FrameNet provides sense definitions, either taken from the Concise Oxford Dictionary or created by lexicographers. Furthermore, there is a sense definition for each frame, which is given by a textual description and shared by all senses in a frame.

- **Sense examples**—FrameNet is particularly rich in sense examples which are selected based on lexicographic criteria.

- **Sense relations**—FrameNet specifies sense relations on the frame level, i.e., all senses in a frame participate in the relation.

- **Predicate argument structure information**—Semantic roles often have frame-specific names and are specified via a textual description. Some frame elements are further characterized via their semantic type, thus selectional preference information is provided as well.

1.1.3   VALENCY LEXICONS

Most of the early work on LKBs for NLP considered valency as a central information type, because it was essential for deep syntactic and semantic parsing with broad-coverage hand-written grammars (e.g., Head-Driven Phrase Structure Grammar [Copestake and Flickinger], or Lexical Functional Grammar as in the ParGram project [Sulger et al., 2013]). Valency is a lexical property of a word to require certain syntactic arguments in order to be used in well-formed phrases or clauses. For example, the verb *assassinate* requires not only a subject, but also an object: **He assassinated.* vs. *He assassinated his colleague.* Valency information is also included in MRDs, but often represented ambiguously and thus is hard to process automatically. Therefore, a number of valency LKBs have been built specifically for NLP applications. These LKBs use subcat frames to represent valency information.

It is important to note that subcat frames are a lexical property of senses, rather than words. Consider the following example of the two senses of *see* and their sense-specific subcat frames (1)

---

[6]http://spanishfn.org
[7]http://spraakbanken.gu.se/eng/swefn
[8]http://jfn.st.hc.keio.ac.jp

and (2): subcat frame (1) is only valid for the *see*—"interpret in a particular way" sense, but not for the *see*—"perceive with the eyes" sense:

> *see*—"interpret in a particular way:"
> subcat frame (1): (arg1:subject(nounPhrase),arg2:prepositionalObject(asPhrase))
> sense example: *Some historians see his usurpation as a panic response to growing insecurity.*

> *see*—"perceive with the eyes:"
> subcat frame (2): (arg1:subject(nounPhrase),arg2:object(nounPhrase))
> sense example: *Can you see the bird in that tree?*

Subcat frames contain language-specific elements, even though some of their elements may be valid cross-lingually. For example, there are certain properties of syntactic arguments in English and German that correspond (both English and German are Germanic languages and hence closely related), while other properties, mainly morphosyntactic ones, diverge [Eckle-Kohler and Gurevych, 2012]. Examples of such divergences include the overt case marking in German (e.g., for the dative case) or the fact that the *ing*-form in English verb phrase complements is sometimes realized as *zu*-infinitive in German.

According to many researchers in linguistics, different subcat frames of a lexeme are associated with different but related meanings, an analysis which is called the "multiple meaning approach" by Hovav and Levin [2008].[9] The multiple meaning approach gives rise to different senses, i.e., pairs of lexeme and subcat frame. Hence, valency LKBs provide an implicit characterization of senses via subcat frames, which can be considered as abstractions of sense examples. Sense examples illustrating a lexeme in a particular subcat frame (e.g., extracted from corpora) might be provided in addition. However, valency LKBs do not necessarily assign unique identifiers to senses, or group (nearly) synonymous senses into entries (as MRDs do).

Examples of Valency Lexicons   COMLEX Syntax is an English valency LKB providing detailed subcat frames for about 38,000 headwords [Grishman et al., 1994]. Another well-known valency LKB is CELEX, which covers English, as well as Dutch and German. The PAROLE project (Preparatory Action for Linguistic Resources Organization for Language Engineering), initiated the creation of valency LKBs in 12 European languages (Catalan, Danish, Dutch, English, Finnish, French, German, Greek, Italian, Portuguese, Spanish and Swedish), which have all been built on the basis of corpora. However, the resulting LKBs are much smaller. For example, the Spanish PAROLE lexicon contains syntactic information for only about 325 verbs [Villegas and Bel, 2015].

There are many valency LKBs in languages other than English. For German, an example of a large-scale valency LKB is IMSLex-Subcat, a broad-coverage subcategorization lexicon for German verbs, nouns and adjectives, covering about 10,000 verbs, 4,000 nouns, and 200 adjectives

---

[9]In contrast, the "single meaning approach" assumes that both subcat frames are associated with the same meaning, with this meaning allowing two syntactic realization options [Hovav and Levin, 2008].

[Eckle-Kohler, 1999, Fitschen, 2004]. For verbs, about 350 different subcat frames are distinguished. IMSLex-Subcat was semi-automatically created: the subcat frames were automatically extracted from large newspaper corpora, and manually filtered afterward.

Information Types   In summary, the following lexical information types are salient for valency LKBs.

- **Syntactic behavior**—Valency LKBs provide lexical-syntactic information on predicate-like words by specifying their syntactic behavior via subcat frames.

- **Sense examples**—For individual pairs of lexeme and subcat frame, sense examples might be given as well.

1.1.4   VERBNETS

According to Levin [1993], verbs that share common syntactic argument alternation patterns also have particular meaning components in common, thus they can be grouped into semantic verb classes. Consider as an example verbs participating in the dative alternation, e.g., *give* and *sell*. These verbs can realize one of their arguments syntactically either as a noun phrase or as a prepositional phrase with *to*, i.e., they can be used with two different subcat frames:

> *Martha gives (sells) an apple to Myrna.*
> *Martha gives (sells) Myrna an apple.*

Verbs having this alternation behavior in common can be grouped into a semantic class of verbs sharing the particular meaning component "change of possession," thus this shared meaning component characterizes the semantic class.

The most well-known verb classification based on the correspondence between verb syntax and verb meaning is Levin's classification of English verbs [Levin, 1993]. Recent work on verb semantics provides additional evidence for this correspondence of verb syntax and meaning [Hartshorne et al., 2014, Levin, 2015].

The English VerbNet [Kipper et al., 2008] is a broad-coverage verb lexicon based on Levin's classification covering about 3,800 verb lemmas. VerbNet is organized in about 270 verb classes based on syntactic alternations. Verbs with common subcat frames and syntactic alternation behavior that also share common semantic roles are grouped into VerbNet classes, which are hierarchically structured to represent information about related subcat frames.

VerbNet not only includes the verbs from the original verb classification by Levin, but also more than 50 additional verb classes [Kipper et al., 2006] automatically acquired from corpora [Korhonen and Briscoe, 2004]. These classes cover many verbs taking non-finite verb phrases and subordinate clauses as complements, which were not included in Levin's original classification. VerbNet (version 3.1) lists 568 subcat frames specifying syntactic types and semantic roles of the arguments, as well as selectional preferences, and syntactic and morpho-syntactic restrictions on the arguments.

Although it might often be hard to pin down what the shared meaning components of VerbNet classes really are, VerbNet has successfully been used in various NLP tasks, many of them including the subtask of mapping syntactic chunks of a sentence to semantic roles [Pradet et al., 2014]; see also Chapter 6.1 for an example.

Verbnets in Other Languages   While the importance of having a verbnet-like LKB in less-resourced languages has been widely recognized, there have rarely been any efforts to build such high-quality verbnets as the English one. Most previous work explored fully automatic approaches to transfer the English VerbNet to another language, thus introducing noise. Semi-automatic approaches are also often based on translating the English VerbNet into another language.

Most importantly, many of the detailed subcat frames available for English, as well as the syntactic alternations, cannot be carried over to other languages, since valency is largely language-specific (e.g., [Scarton and Aluísio, 2012]). Therefore, the development of high-quality verbnets in languages other than English requires the existence of a broad-coverage valency lexicon as a prerequisite. For this reason, valency lexicons, especially tools for their (semi-)automatic construction, are still receiving considerable attention.

A recent example of a high-quality verbnet in another language is the French verbnet (covering about 2,000 verb lemmas) [Pradet et al., 2014] which has been built semi-automatically from existing French resources (thus also including subcat frames) combined with a translation of the English VerbNet verbs.

Information Types   We summarize the main lexical information types for senses present in the English VerbNet.

- **Sense definition**—Verbnets do not provide textual sense definitions. A verb sense is defined extensionally by the set of verbs forming a VerbNet class; the verbs share common subcat frames, as well as semantic roles and selectional preferences of their arguments.

- **Sense relations**—The verb classes in verbnets are organized hierarchically and the subclass relation is therefore defined on the verb class level.

- **Syntactic behavior**—VerbNet lists detailed subcat frames for verb senses.

- **Predicate argument structure information**—In the English VerbNet, each individual verb sense is characterized by a semi-formal semantic predicate based on the event decomposition of Moens and Steedman [1988]. Furthermore, the semantic arguments of a verb are characterized by their semantic role and linked to their syntactic counterparts in the subcat frame. Most semantic arguments are additionally characterized by their semantic type (i.e., selectional preference information).

1.2   COLLABORATIVELY CONSTRUCTED KNOWLEDGE BASES

More recently, the rapid development of Web technologies and especially collaborative participation channels (often labeled "Web 2.0") has offered new possibilities for the construction of
language resources. The basic idea is that, instead of a small group of experts, a community of users
("crowd") collaboratively gathers and edits the lexical information in an open and equitable process. The resulting knowledge is in turn also free to use, adapt and extend for everyone. This open
approach has turned out to be very promising to handle the enormous effort of building language
resources, as a large community can quickly adapt to new language phenomena like neologisms
while at the same time maintaining a high quality by continuous revision—a phenomenon which
has become known as the "wisdom of crowds" [Surowiecki, 2005]. The approach also seems to be
suitable for multilingual resources, as users speaking any language and from any culture can easily contribute. This is very helpful for minor, usually resource-poor languages where expert-built
resources are small or not available at all.

1.2.1   WIKIPEDIA

Wikipedia[10] is a collaboratively constructed online encyclopedia and one of the largest freely
available knowledge sources. It has long surpassed traditional printed encyclopedias in size, while
maintaining a comparative quality [Giles, 2005]. The current English version contains around
4,700,000 articles and is by far the largest one, while there are many language editions of significant size. Some, like the German or French editions, also contain more than 1,000,000 articles,
each of which usually describes a particular concept.

Although Wikipedia has not been designed as a sense inventory, we can interpret the pairing of an article title and the concept described in the article text as a sense. This interpretation
is in accordance with the disambiguation provided in Wikipedia, either as part of the title or on
separate disambiguation pages. An example of the former are some articles for *Java* where its
different meanings are marked by "bracketed disambiguations" in the article title such as *Java
(programming language)* and *Java (town)*. An example of the latter is the dedicated disambiguation page for *Java* which explicitly lists all *Java* senses contained in Wikipedia.

Due to its focus on encyclopedic knowledge, Wikipedia almost exclusively contains nouns.
Similar as for word senses, the interpretation of Wikipedia as a LKB gives rise to the induction
of further lexical information types, such as sense relations of translations. Since the original
purpose of Wikipedia is not to serve as a LKB, this induction process might also lead to inaccurate
lexical information. For instance, the links to corresponding articles in other languages provided
for Wikipedia articles can be used to derive translations (i.e., equivalents) of an article "sense"
into other languages. An example where this leads to an inaccurate translation is the English
article *Vanilla extract* which links to a subsection titled *Vanilleextrakt* within the German article

---

[10]http://www.wikipedia.org

Vanille (Gewürz); according to our lexical interpretation of Wikipedia, this leads to the inaccurate German equivalent *Vanille (Gewürz)* for *Vanilla extract*.

Nevertheless, Wikipedia is commonly used as a lexical resource in computational linguistics where it was introduced as such by Zesch et al. [2007], and has subsequently been used for knowledge mining [Erdmann et al., 2009, Medelyan et al., 2009] and various other tasks [Gurevych and Kim, 2012].

Information Types   We can derive the following lexical information types from Wikipedia.

- **Sense definition**—While by design one article describes one particular concept, the first paragraph of an article usually gives a concise summary of the concept, which can therefore fulfill the role of a sense definition for NLP purposes.

- **Sense examples**—While usage examples are not explicitly encoded in Wikipedia, they are also inferable by considering the Wikipedia link structure. If a term is linked within an article, the surrounding sentence can be considered as a usage example for the target concept of the link.

- **Sense relations**—Related articles, i.e., senses, are connected via hyperlinks within the article text. However, since the type of the relation is usually missing, these hyperlinks cannot be considered full-fledged sense relations. Nevertheless, they express a certain degree of semantic relatedness. The same observation holds for the Wikipedia category structure which links articles belonging to particular domains.

- **Equivalents**—The different language editions of Wikipedia are interlinked at the article level—the article titles in other languages can thus be used as translation equivalents.

Related Projects   As Wikipedia has nowadays become one of the largest and most widely used knowledge sources, there have been numerous efforts to make it better accessible for automatic processing. These include projects such as YAGO [Suchanek et al., 2007], DBPedia [Bizer et al., 2009], WikiNet [Nastase et al., 2010], MENTA [de Melo and Weikum, 2010], or DBPedia [Bizer et al., 2009]. Most of them aim at deriving a concept network from Wikipedia ("ontologizing") and making it available for Semantic Web applications. WikiData,[11]—a project directly rooted in Wikimedia—has similar goals, but within the framework given by Wikipedia. The goal here is to provide a language-independent repository of structured world knowledge, which all language editions can easily integrate.

These related projects basically contain the same knowledge as Wikipedia, only in a different representation format (e.g., suitable for Semantic Web applications), hence we will not discuss them further in this chapter. However, some of the Wikipedia derivatives have reached a wide audience in different communities, including NLP (e.g., DBPedia), and have also been used in different linking efforts, especially in the domain of ontology construction. We will describe corresponding efforts in Chapter 2

---

[11]http://www.wikidata.org

1.2.2   WIKTIONARY

Wiktionary[12] is a dictionary "side project" of Wikipedia that was created in order to better cater for the need to represent specific lexicographic knowledge, which is not well suited for an encyclopedia, e.g., lexical knowledge about verbs and adjectives. Wiktionary is available in over 500 languages, and currently the English edition of Wiktionary contains almost 4,000,000 lexical entry pages, while many other language editions achieve a considerable size of over 100,000 entries. Meyer and Gurevych [2012b] found that the collaborative construction approach of Wiktionary yields language versions covering the majority of language families and regions of the world, and that it especially covers a vast amount of domain-specific descriptions not found in wordnets for these languages.

For each lexeme, multiple senses can be encoded, and these are usually described by glosses. Wiktionary contains hyperlinks which lead to semantically related lexemes, such as synonyms, hypernyms, or meronyms, and provides a variety of other information types such as etymology or translations to other languages. However, the link targets are not disambiguated in all language editions, e.g., in the English edition, the links merely lead to pages for the lexical entries, which is problematic for NLP applications as we will see later on. The ambiguity of the links is due to the fact that Wiktionary has been primarily designed to be used by humans rather than machines. The entries are thus formatted for easy perception using appropriate font sizes and bold, italic, or colored text styles. In contrast, for machines, data needs to be available in a structured and unambiguous manner in order to become directly accessible. For instance, an easily accessible data structure for machines would be a list of all translations of a given sense, and encoding the translations by their corresponding sense identifiers in the target language LKBs would make the representation unambiguous.

This kind of explicit and unambiguous structure does not exist in Wiktionary, but needs to be inferred from the wiki markup.[13] Although there are guidelines on how to properly structure a Wiktionary entry, Wiktionary editors are permitted to choose from multiple variants or to deviate from the standards if this can enhance the entry. This presents a major challenge for the automatic processing of Wiktionary data. Another hurdle is the openness of Wiktionary—that is, the possibility to perform structural changes at any time, which raises the need for constant revision of the extraction software.

Wiktionary as a resource for NLP has been introduced by Zesch et al. [2008b], and has been considered in many different contexts in subsequent work [Gurevych and Wolf, 2010, Krizhanovsky, 2012, Meyer, 2013, Meyer and Gurevych, 2010, 2012b]. While much work on Wiktionary specifically focuses on few selected language editions, the multilingual LKB Dbnary by Sérasset and Tchechmedjiev [2014] has taken a much broader approach and derived a LKB

---

[12]http://www.wiktionary.org

[13]Wiki markup is an annotation language consisting of a set of special characters and keywords that can be used to mark headlines, bold and italic text styles, tables, hyperlinks, etc. within the article. The four equality signs in "====Translations====" denote, for example, a small headline that usually precedes the list of a word's translations. This markup can be used by a software tool to identify the beginning of the translation section, which supposedly looks similar on each article page.

from Wiktionary editions in 12 languages. A major goal of DBnary is to make Wiktionary easily accessible for automatic processing, especially in Semantic Web applications [Sérasset, 2015].

Particularly interesting for this book are the recent efforts to ontologize Wiktionary and transform it into a standard-compliant, machine-readable format [Meyer and Gurevych, 2012a]. These efforts address issues which are also relevant for the construction of Linked Lexical Knowledge Bases (LLKBs) we will discuss later on. We refer the interested reader to Meyer [2013] for an in-depth survey of Wiktionary from a lexicographic perspective and as a resource for NLP.

Information Types   In summary, the main information types contained in Wiktionary are as follows.

- **Sense definition**—Glosses are given for the majority of senses, but due to the open editing approach gaps or "stub" definitions are explicitly allowed. This is especially the case for smaller language editions.

- **Sense examples**—Example sentences which illustrate the usage of a sense are given for a subset of senses.

- **Sense relations**—As mentioned above, semantic relations are generally available, but depending on the language edition, these might be ambiguously encoded. Moreover, different language editions show a great variety of the amount of relations relative to the number of senses. For instance, the German edition is six times more densely linked than the English one.

- **Syntactic behavior**—Lexical-syntactic properties are given for a small set of senses. These include subcat frame labels, such as "transitive" or "intransitive."

- **Related forms**—Related forms are available via links.

- **Equivalents**—As for Wikipedia, translations of senses to other languages are available by links to other language editions. An interesting peculiarity of Wiktionary is that distinct language editions may also contain entries for foreign-language words, for instance, the English edition also contains German lexemes, complete with definitions etc. in English. This is meant as an aid for language learners and is frequently used.

- **Sense links**—Many Wiktionary entries contain links to the corresponding Wikipedia page, thus providing an easy means to supply additional knowledge about a particular concept without overburdening Wiktionary with non-essential (i.e., encyclopedic) information.

In general, it has to be noted that the flexibility of Wiktionary enables the encoding of all kinds of linguistic knowledge, at least in theory. In practice, the information types listed here are those which are commonly used, and thus interesting for our subsequent considerations.

1.2.3 OMEGAWIKI

OmegaWiki,[14] like Wiktionary, is freely editable via its web frontend. The current version of OmegaWiki contains over 46,000 concepts and lexicalizations in almost 500 languages. One of OmegaWiki's discriminating features, in comparison to other collaboratively constructed resources, is that it is based on a fixed database structure which users have to comply with [Matuschek and Gurevych, 2011]. It was initiated in 2006 and explicitly designed with the goal of offering structured and consistent access to lexical information, i.e., avoiding the shortcomings of Wiktionary described above.

To this end, the creators of OmegaWiki decided to limit the degrees of freedom for contributors by providing a "scaffold" of elements which interact in well-defined ways. The central elements of OmegaWiki's organizational structure are language-independent concepts (so-called *defined meanings*) to which lexicalizations of the concepts are attached. Defined meanings can thus be considered as multilingual synsets, comparable to resources such as WordNet (cf. Section 1.1.1). Consequently, no specific language editions exist for OmegaWiki as they do for Wiktionary. Rather, all multilingual information is encoded in a single resource.

As an example, defined meaning no. 5616 (representing the concept HAND) carries the lexicalizations *hand*, *main*, *mano*, etc., and also definitions in different languages which describe this concept, for example, "That part of the fore limb below the forearm or wrist." The multilingual synsets directly yield correct translations as these are merely different lexicalizations of the same concept. It is also possible to have multiple lexicalizations in the same language, i.e., synonyms. An interesting consequence of this design, especially for multilingual applications, is that semantic relations are defined between concepts regardless of existing lexicalizations. Consider, for example, the Spanish noun *dedo*: it is marked as hypernym of *finger* and *toe*, although there exists no corresponding lexicalization for the defined meaning FINGER OR TOE in English. This is, for instance, immediately helpful in translation tasks, since concepts for which no lexicalization in the target language exists can be described or replaced by closely related concepts. Using this kind of information is not as straightforward as in other multilingual resources like Wiktionary, because the links are not necessarily unambiguous.

The fixed structure of OmegaWiki ensures easy extraction of the information due to the consistency enforced by the definition of database tables and relations between them. However, it has the drawback of limited expressiveness, for instance, the coding of grammatical properties is only possible to a small extent. In OmegaWiki, the users are not allowed to extend this structure and thus are tied to what has been already defined. Consequently, OmegaWiki's lack of flexibility and extensibility, in combination with the fact that Wiktionary was already quite popular at its creation time, has caused the OmegaWiki community to remain rather small. While OmegaWiki had 6,746 users at the time of writing, only 19 of them had actively been editing in the past month, i.e., the community is considerably smaller than for Wikipedia or Wiktionary [Meyer, 2013]. Despite the above-mentioned issues, we still believe that OmegaWiki is not only interesting for

---

[14]http://www.omegawiki.org

usage in NLP applications (and thereby for integration into LLKBs), but also as a case study, since it exemplifies how the process of collaboratively creating a large-scale lexical-semantic resource can be guided by means of a structural "skeleton."

Information Types   The most salient information types in OmegaWiki, i.e., those encoded in a relevant portion of entries are as follows.

- **Sense definitions**—Glosses are provided on the concept level, usually in multiple languages.

- **Sense examples**—Examples are given for individual lexicalizations, but only for a few of them.

- **Sense relations**—Semantic as well as ontological relations (e.g., "Germany" borders on "France") are given, and these are entirely disambiguated.

- **Equivalents**—Translations are encoded by the multilingual synsets which group lexicalizations of a concept in different languages.

- **Sense links**—As for Wiktionary, mostly links to related Wikipedia articles are given to provide more background knowledge about particular concepts.

1.3   STANDARDS

Since LKBs play an important role in many NLP tasks and are expensive to build, the capability to exchange, reuse, and also merge them has become a major requirement. Standardization of LKBs plays an important role in this context, because it allows to build uniform APIs, and thus facilitates exchange and reuse, as well as integration and merging of LKBs. Moreover, applications can easily switch between different standardized LKBs.

1.3.1   ISO LEXICAL MARKUP FRAMEWORK

The ISO standard Lexical Markup Framework (LMF) [Calzolari et al., 2013, Francopoulo and George, 2013, ISO24613, 2008] was developed to address these issues. LMF is an abstract standard, it defines a *meta-model* of lexical resources, covering both NLP lexicons and machine readable dictionaries. The standard specifies this meta-model in the Unified Modeling Language (UML) by providing a set of UML diagrams. UML packages are used to organize the meta-model and each diagram given in the standard corresponds to an UML package. LMF defines a mandatory core package and a number of extension packages for different types of resources, e.g., morphological resources or wordnets. The core package models a lexicon in the traditional headword-based fashion, i.e., organized by lexical entries. Each lexical entry is defined as the pairing of one to many forms and zero to many senses.

The abstract meta-model given by the LMF standard is not immediately usable as a format for encoding (i.e., converting) an existing LKB [Tokunaga et al., 2009]. It has to be instantiated first, i.e., a full-fledged lexicon model has to be developed by choosing LMF classes and by specifying suitable attributes for these LMF classes.

According to the standard, developing a lexicon model involves

1. *selecting* LMF extension packages (the usage of the core package is mandatory),

2. *defining* attributes for the classes in the core package and in the extension packages (as they are not prescribed by the standard), and

3. *explicating* the linguistic terminology, i.e., linking the attributes and other linguistic terms introduced (e.g., attribute values) to standardized descriptions of their meaning.

Selecting a combination of LMF classes and their relationships from the LMF core package and from the extension packages establishes the structure of a lexicon model. While the LMF core package models a lexicon in terms of lexical entries, the LMF extensions provide classes for different types of lexicon organization, e.g., covering the synset-based organization of wordnets or the semantic frame-based organization of FrameNet.

Fixing the structure of a lexicon model by choosing a set of classes contributes to the interoperability of LKBs, as it determines the high-level organization of lexical knowledge in a resource, e.g., whether synonymy is encoded by grouping senses into synsets (using the `Synset` class) or by specifying sense relations (using the `SenseRelation` class), which connect synonymous senses (i.e., synonyms). Defining attributes for the LMF classes and specifying the attribute values is far more challenging than choosing from a given set of classes, because the standard gives only a few examples of attributes and leaves the specification of attributes to the user in order to allow maximum flexibility.

Finally, the attributes and values have to be linked to a description of their meaning in an ISO compliant Data Category Registry [ISO12620, 2009, Windhouwer and Wright, 2013]. For example, ISOcat[15] was the first implementation of the ISO Data Category Registry standard [ISO12620, 2009].[16] The data model defined by the Data Category Registry specifies some mandatory information types for its entries, including a unique administrative identifier (e.g., `partOfSpeech`) and a unique and persistent identifier (PID, e.g., `http://www.isocat.org/dat cat/DC-396`) which can be used in automatic processing and annotation, in order to link to the entries. From a practical point of view, a Data Category Registry can be considered as a repository of mostly linguistic terminology which provides human-readable descriptions of the meaning of terms used in language resources. For instance, the meaning of many terms used for linguistic annotation is given in ISOcat, such as *grammaticalNumber, gender, case*. Accordingly, a Data Category Registry can be used as a glossary: users can look up the meaning of a term occurring in a language resource by consulting its entry in the Data Category Registry.

---

[15]`www.isocat.org`

[16]ISOcat has been shut down and currently only a static dump of ISOcat is accessible at `www.isocat.org`. A successor of ISOcat is the OpenSKOS-based CLARIN Concept Registry (`https://openskos.meertens.knaw.nl/ccr/browser`). In addition, a relaunch of ISOcat is planned by the ISO TC37 community.

Data Category Registries, such as ISOcat, play an important role in making language resources *semantically interoperable* [Ide and Pustejovsky, 2010]. Semantically interoperable language resources share a common definition of their linguistic vocabulary, for instance, the linguistic terms used in a LKB. LKBs can be made semantically interoperable by connecting these terms with their meaning defined externally in a Data Category Registry. Consider as an example the `LexicalEntry` class of two different lexicon models A and B. Lexicon model A may have an attribute `partOfSpeech` (POS), while lexicon model B may have an attribute `pos`. Linking both attributes to the ISOcat entry with the meaning "A category assigned to a word based on its grammatical and semantic properties." (see `http://www.isocat.org/datcat/DC-396`) makes the two lexicon models semantically interoperable with respect to the POS attribute. Thus, a human can look up the meaning of a term occurring in a lexicon model by following the link to the ISOCat entry and consulting its description. Linking the attributes and their values in an LMF lexicon model to ISOCat entries results in a so-called Data Category Selection. It is important to stress that the notion of "semantic interoperability" in the context of LMF has a limited scope: it only refers to the meaning of the linguistic vocabulary used in an LMF lexicon model—not to the meaning of the lexemes listed in a LKB.

Instantiations of LMF   Various LMF lexicon models have been developed and populated with data from LKBs, mostly for a single type of LKB, such as wordnets [Henrich and Hinrichs, 2010, Lee et al., Soria et al., 2009, Toral et al., 2010a, Vossen et al., 2013], or machine readable dictionaries [Attia et al., 2010, Khemakhem et al., 2013].

Considering the fact that only a fleshed-out LMF lexicon model, i.e., an instantiation of the LMF standard, can be used for actually standardizing LKBs, it is obvious that independently created LMF-compliant LKBs are not necessarily interoperable. This issue is addressed by UBY-LMF [Eckle-Kohler et al., 2012, 2013], a large-scale instantiation of ISO LMF which can be applied to the whole range of LKB types introduced in the previous sections. UBY-LMF has been designed as a uniform format for standardizing both expert-constructed resources—wordnets, FrameNet, VerbNet—and collaboratively constructed resources—Wikipedia, Wiktionary, OmegaWiki. The full UBY-LMF model consists of 39 classes and 129 attributes. UBY-LMF provides a fine-grained instantiation of the LMF Syntax extension classes in order to cover detailed verb subcategorization frames present, e.g., in VerbNet. UBY-LMF provides a harmonized subcategorization frame format across two languages, English and German. This format enables a modular specification of subcategorization frames by a number of attributes that are uniform across English and German. All syntactic arguments are specified by the attributes `grammaticalFunction` and `syntacticCategory`. A number of morphosyntactic attributes allow a fine-grained specification of different phrase types. While most of the attribute values are uniform across English and German, there are four morphosyntactic attributes that can take language-specific values. Details on this uniform format for subcategorization frames in English and German can be found in Eckle-Kohler and Gurevych [2012].

1.3.2 SEMANTIC WEB STANDARDS

The Semantic Web [Berners-Lee et al., 2001] can be considered as a huge data integration platform since the use of the Resource Description Framework (RDF) supports data integration and offers a large body of tools for accessing this data. There has been significant work toward integrating LKBs using RDF and linked data principles [Chiarcos et al., 2013]. Most notably, the use of publicly accessible unique identifiers (URIs) for information types represented in RDF allows different and distributed LKBs to link to each other.

Many LKBs have been made available in this way (e.g., WordNet, Wikipedia [Bizer et al., 2009], and Wiktionary). While representing LKBs in RDF makes them syntactically interoperable, due to the data structures given by RDF, it does not per se make them semantically interoperable. Consider, for instance, existing conversions of WordNet and FrameNet [Narayanan et al., 2003, Van Assem et al., 2006], where a simple mapping to RDF is augmented with OWL semantics. The formats chosen for these RDF versions of WordNet and FrameNet are different, they are specific to the underlying data models of WordNet and FrameNet—two LKBs which have been characterized as complementary regarding their structure and lexical information types [Baker and Fellbaum, 2009]. Therefore, it is difficult to use the RDF versions of WordNet and FrameNet as interchangeable modules in NLP applications.

In order to overcome this difficulty, the *lemon* lexicon model [McCrae et al., 2011, 2012a] was proposed as a common interchange format for lexical resources on the Semantic Web. *lemon* realizes a separation of lexicon and ontology layers, so that *lemon* lexica can be linked to existing ontologies in the linked data cloud.[17] *lemon* has its historical roots in LMF and thus allows easy conversion from LKBs standardized according to LMF. Like LMF lexicon models, *lemon* refers to data categories in linguistic terminology repositories (such as the ISO Data Category Registry). *lemon* has been used to represent various LKBs, e.g., Wiktionary [Sérasset, 2015] and several LKBs rich both in subcategorization frames and semantic information types [Del Gratta et al., 2015, Villegas and Bel, 2015]. It has also been used as a basis for integrating the data of the English Wiktionary with the RDF version of WordNet [McCrae et al., 2012b].

1.4 CHAPTER CONCLUSION

This chapter set out a definition of LKB which we will use in all subsequent chapters of this book. Building on this definition we introduced seven major "kinds" of LKBs frequently used in NLP:

- wordnets (i.e., the Princeton WordNet and its spin-offs in other languages);

- framenets (i.e., the Berkeley FrameNet and its spin-offs in other languages);

- valency lexicons;

- verbnets (i.e., the English VerbNet and its spin-offs in other languages);

---

[17]More detail of the model can be found at `http://lemon-model.net`

- Wikipedia and Wiktionary as collaborative LKBs with editions in many languages; and

- the multilingual wordnet OmegaWiki, a collaborative LKB as well.

All these kinds of LKBs are structured and organized differently, and cover different information types. Table 1.1 provides an overview of the major information types[18] covered by the seven LKB types.

Table 1.1: Overview of information types covered by different kinds of LKBs: wordnets (WN), framenets (FN), valency lexicons (VL), verbnets (VN), Wikipedia (WP), Wiktionary (WKT), and OmegaWiki (OW)

Information Type	WN	FN	VL	VN	WP	WKT	OW
Sense Definition	x	x	-	-	x	x	x
Sense Examples	x	x	-	-	-	x	-
Sense Relations	x	x	-	-	x	x	x
Syntactic Behavior	x	-	x	x	-	x	-
Predicate Argument Structure Information	-	x	-	x	-	-	-
Related Forms	x	-	-	-	-	x	-
Equivalents	-	-	-	-	x	x	x
Sense Links	-	-	-	-	-	x	x

This overview might convey a first impression of the complexity of linking different LKBs at the sense level.

Our concluding summary of major standards for LKBs plays a subordinate role in the context of this book. We included it because many of the above-listed LKBs have been standardized, some of them especially in the context of linking.

---

[18]By "major" we mean those information types which are attached to a substantial number of senses in a LKB.

CHAPTER 2

Linked Lexical Knowledge Bases

In this chapter, we move closer to the core of this book: the *linking* of LKBs. To this end, we first have to formally define what this linking means, and especially at what level it is taking place.

Definition <u>Word Sense Linking:</u>   We define one instance of a Word Sense Linking (WSL), or also Word Sense Alignment (WSA),[1] as a list of pairs of senses (or, more generally, concepts) from two LKBs, where the members of each pair represent an equivalent meaning.

As an example for this definition, the two senses of the noun *letter* "The conventional characters of the alphabet used to represent speech" and "A symbol in an alphabet, bookstave" (taken from WordNet and Wiktionary, respectively) are clearly equivalent and should thus be aligned. Note that our definition is not necessarily restricted to 1:1 alignments, i.e., a sense may participate in more than one pair, so it is possible that one sense s is assigned to several other senses $t_1, \ldots, t_n$, in case the sense distinctions have different granularities in different LKBs.

Based on this definition on the sense level, we can move on to the second definition.

Definition <u>Linked Lexical Knowledge Base:</u>   A linked lexical knowledge base (LLKB) is a set consisting of at least two LKBs, where for each LKB there exists a non-empty subset of its senses participating in a word sense linking with another LKB.

Less formally, two LKBs form a LLKB if there exists at least one sense linking between them. If more than two LKBs participate, it is not strictly necessary to have a pairwise linking between each of them—though if this is the case, we can speak of a *fully linked* LLKB. It is important to note at this point that this "full linking" only makes a statement at the resource level, not at the sense level. Consider again the example of two LKBs which share at least one sense linking: these can be considered a fully linked LLKB by definition, but this does by no means imply that all of the *senses* are participating in the linking. As a matter of fact, due to the different coverage of concepts in resources, it is most unlikely for a resource pair that a (correct) sense linking can be found which encompasses all senses.

---

[1]Note that in related work the terms *sense mapping* and *sense matching* are also used. Sense alignment should, however, not be confused with *word alignment*, which takes place at the lexical level and is a preprocessing step in machine translation.

In the remainder of this chapter, we will discuss different examples of LLKBs, considering the motivation for their creation, the choice of resources involved, and other noteworthy characteristics. This chapter does not go into detail regarding algorithms for automatic linking and methods for applying LLKBs in NLP, as these aspects will be covered at length in Chapters 3 and 4. Note that we will not describe linked LLKBs on the Semantic Web in detail. Mostly, these are existing resources which are converted into a Semantic Web format; however, the basic principles and algorithms used for linking (see next chapter) stay the same.

2.1   COMBINING LKBS FOR SPECIFIC TASKS

In NLP, the combination of LKBs has been investigated for more than twenty years, and much work aimed at improving the performance of particular NLP tasks. An early work by Knight and Luk [1994] aligns WordNet to the *Longman Dictionary of Contemporary English* (LDOCE) in order to provide more background knowledge for machine translation.

Jing and McKeown [1998] combine several expert-built resources for the purpose of Natural Language Generation. They combine WordNet, Levin's verb classes, the COMLEX syntax dictionary, as well as the Brown Corpus in a rule-based approach.

King and Crouch [2005] combine WordNet, VerbNet and the Cyc ontology (providing everyday common sense knowledge [Reed and Lenat, 2002]) in order to create knowledge representations from text. Their knowledge representations cover the correspondence of syntax and semantics made available through the combination of VerbNet on the one hand, and WordNet and Cyc on the other hand.

Shi and Mihalcea [2005] present a semi-automatic linking algorithm for FrameNet, VerbNet and WordNet for improving semantic parsing. Navigli [2006] creates a linking between WordNet and the *Oxford Dictionary of English* (ODE) in order to create a coarse-grained version of WordNet for enhanced Word Sense Disambiguation (WSD). Improving WSD by the means of richer sense representations is also the goal of Mihalcea [2007] who manually link WordNet and Wikipedia.

For the purpose of verb classification in cognitive linguistics research, Chow and Webster [2007] present a combination of FrameNet, WordNet and *SUMO* (Suggested Upper Merged Ontology [Niles and Pease, 2001]).

With the rise of collaboratively constructed knowledge sources in recent years, and more and more proof of their usefulness in NLP applications, different attempts have been made to combine them with expert-built resources at a large scale. One early suggestion is the freely available *NULEX* [McFate and Forbus, 2011], which integrates WordNet, VerbNet, and Wiktionary. It was automatically created with the purpose to enhance syntactic parsing. For this reason, NULEX only covers selected information types relevant for syntactic parsing—for instance, from Wiktionary, NULEX includes certain grammatical information types which are not covered in the other resources.

2.2   LARGE-SCALE LLKBS

The pinnacle of the idea of combining different resources (and especially different kinds of resources), and the current state-of-the-art, is to automatically create a linking between more than two of them, in order to achieve the best possible coverage and richness of knowledge types for a variety of different NLP tasks. In this section, we discuss the challenges of this approach and give a more detailed comparison of the currently predominant players.

One of the main challenges for creating these large-scale linkings is the consistent matching of different information types. While this can be difficult for two resources, matching three or more of them often requires relaxed assumptions regarding the interpretation and linking as an exact match is rarely possible—this is also the reason why, besides some rather unsuccessful attempts [Kirschner, 2012, Matuschek, 2014], matching of several resources at once is not viable, as the room for interpretation and thus the possible error propagation is unacceptable. The more common approach is to align the resources in a pairwise fashion (which is a reasonably well-understood problem, see the following sections), and then construct more complex alignments based on this.

Another issue with creating a linking between several resources is the lexical coverage—in several studies in the past, it has been confirmed that, while the overlap between two resources can be reasonably high, the more resources are involved, the fewer lexical items lie in the intersection of all of them [Meyer and Gurevych, 2010, Miller and Gurevych, 2014]. Depending on the combination of resources, it is possible that only a few thousand (or even hundred) items are completely covered, which might not be sufficient depending on the particular application scenario.

UBY [Gurevych et al., 2012a] is a large-scale attempt at resource integration. It combines the English WordNet, Wiktionary, Wikipedia, FrameNet, VerbNet, German Wikipedia, Wiktionary, GermaNet, OpenThesaurus, the German valency lexicon IMSLex-Subcat, as well as the multilingual OmegaWiki. Apart from the numerous sense linkings for a large subset of the resources, a distinguishing feature of UBY is that it provides standardized and hence interoperable versions of the LKBs. The structure of UBY and its entries is determined in the Lexical Markup Framework (LMF)-based model [Francopoulo et al., 2009] UBY-LMF which we have introduced in the previous chapter. The data model UBY-LMF has been designed to capture all information types available in the integrated resources, i.e., UBY can be considered the *union* of all its resources. Accompanying UBY, there are also a Java-based API and a web interface available. UBY has, for instance, successfully been used in distantly supervised learning for verb sense disambiguation [Cholakov et al., 2014].

The other popular and comprehensive approach to resource integration nowadays, which is especially rich in multilingual information, is *BabelNet* [Navigli and Ponzetto, 2012a]. As of 2015, this resource integrates WordNet, *Open Multilingual Wordnet*, a French translation of WordNet (WoNeF), VerbNet, Wikipedia, OmegaWiki, Wiktionary, factual world knowledge from Wikidata, Wikiquote, Microsoft Terminology, GeoNames, and ImageNet. BabelNet uses an underlying data model that captures the *intersection* of all the integrated resources with a focus on translation information, i.e., a BabelNet entry provides only sense definitions and translations into multiple languages, but not subcategorization frames. Translation gaps in the integrated resources have been filled using machine translation. The result is a multilingual network (created for large parts via automated alignment, see Chapter 3) containing about 14 million entries and covering 272 languages; it has been used for tasks such as the creation of semantic predicates [Flati and Navigli, 2013] and semantic relatedness computation [Navigli and Ponzetto, 2012c]. It has also advanced the state-of-the-art in knowledge-based WSD for noun mentions and entity linking [Moro et al., 2014b], and it is part of the *Linguistic Linked Open Data* (LLOD) cloud[2] and hence is also available in a standardized format.

While UBY and BabelNet have at times been considered competitors, this assessment fails to recognize their different (and for the most part, complementary) philosophies. Although they both contain the same resources at the core (for instance, WordNet), BabelNet's early development was primarily based on the alignment of WordNet and Wikipedia, which by the very nature of Wikipedia implied a strong focus on nouns, and especially named entities. Only in its later development the focus was shifted more toward other parts of speech. UBY, on the other hand, was from the start designed to also cover verb information, or more specifically, syntactic information and predicate argument structure information, which is contained in resources such as VerbNet or FrameNet.

The most important difference is that UBY aims at modeling the different resources separately, but completely, so that UBY can be used as a wholesale replacement for each of the contained resources,[3] with the additional benefit of alignments between the resources if they are required. BabelNet, on the other hand, bakes only selected information types[4] into so-called *Babel Synsets*. This approach makes accessing and processing of the lexical knowledge more convenient, but blurs the lines between the integrated LKBs. Moreover, BabelNet also enriches the original resources by adding automatically created translations for concepts which are not lexicalized in a particular language. While this provides a great boost of coverage for multilingual applications (for instance, the one we present later on in Section 6), it has to be kept in mind that automatic inference of information is always prone to a certain degree of error. BabelNet currently does not include provenance information for the translations, although this information could be preserved in principle.[5] Consequently, a user has no way of distinguishing automatically created translations and translations inferred from the interlingual links in Wikipedia.

In summary, both resources have quite different characteristics, so that a usage of one or the other might be preferred depending on the particular application scenario. Considering their open and well-documented structure, it might also be a viable option to create a linking between

---

[2]http://linguistics.okfn.org/resources/llod/
[3]The access to single resources is supported by the API via a single parameter.
[4]Pronunciations from Wiktionary, for instance, are not included.
[5]See https://www.w3.org/community/bpmlod/wiki/Converting_BabelNet_as_Linguistic_Linked_Data accessed on March 30, 2016.

them (especially considering the large overlap in covered resources and hence concepts). This way, the extensive lexicographic knowledge contained within them can be leveraged.

2.3   AUTOMATIC LINKING INVOLVING WORDNETS

The *automatic* linking of LKBs has been particularly well studied for wordnets, as this is the LKB type predominantly used in NLP. In this section, we discuss selected examples of such approaches involving the Princeton WordNet and some of its spin-offs in other languages.

Pairwise Linking of Wordnets and Other LKB Types   Many works linked wordnets with another LKB type, and thus provided the research community with a better understanding of the automatic linking task.

An early proof-of-concept approach to automatically linking the Princeton WordNet to other LKBs was presented by Kwong [1998]. She linked LDOCE to *Roget's Thesaurus* via Word-Net using a notion of similarity between senses based on gloss overlap.

For the alignment of WordNet and domain-thesauri, an approach based on gloss overlap is not applicable, since thesauri usually do not provide glosses. Alternatively, the organization of thesauri into domain concepts (groups of semantically related senses) and their structure (taxonomic relations between domain concepts) can be leveraged for an alignment to WordNet. Burgun and Bodenreider [2001] aligned WordNet to the *Unified Medical Language System* (UMLS) thesaurus using the "term" overlap of WordNet synsets and UMLS domain concepts. Toral et al. [2010b] linked a domain thesaurus to WordNet by exploiting the structural similarity of the semantic networks induced by the sense relations provided by the two resources, i.e., the relations between synsets in WordNet and the taxonomic relations in the domain thesaurus.

There are numerous approaches which automatically align WordNet to Wikipedia. A naive approach was taken in the YAGO (*Yet Another Great Ontology*) [Suchanek et al., 2007, 2008] project. The goal is to build a general knowledge repository for different purposes, and the included WordNet-Wikipedia linking was created using the most frequent sense (MFS) information contained in WordNet. However, the majority of works used some notion of similarity between senses—we will explain the different similarity measures and corresponding algorithms in Chapter 3. Examples include the work by Ruiz-Casado et al. [2005] and De Melo and Weikum [2010] who align WordNet to full Wikipedia articles; the resulting LLKBs *WordNet++* and *Universal WordNet* (UWN) have been used for a considerable number of NLP applications.

The alignment of wordnets with another LKB type has been much less investigated for languages other than English. An interesting LKB type in this context is Wiktionary due to the broad range of information types it provides (depending, of course on the size and coverage of the Wiktionary edition in a particular language). For example, Henrich et al. [2011] link the German wordnet GermaNet and Wiktionary, with the eventual goal of enriching GermaNet with more glosses, as only a fraction of senses originally had a textual description. Bond and Foster [2013] aim to enrich wordnets in many under-resourced languages by aligning them to Wiktionary in the course of the *Open Multilingual Wordnet* project. Both Henrich et al. [2011] and Bond and Foster [2013] determine the similarity of senses based on the overlap between bags-of-words constructed from glosses and semantically related words.

A large body of work has been dedicated to linking WordNet and FrameNet in order to better capture the peculiarities of verb usage. For verbs, the information types provided by WordNet and FrameNet are quite different and can be considered as complementary (also see Chapter 1). As it has long been established that verbs are the most challenging part of speech for tasks such as WSD, it makes sense to tap all available knowledge sources to handle them more effectively. Several different approaches have been considered for solving this task, but most are based on some variation of gloss similarity measures [Baker and Fellbaum, 2009, Ferrandez et al., 2010, Johansson and Nugues, 2007, Laparra and Rigau, 2009, Laparra et al., 2010]. One of the most sophisticated attempts to create such a linking by Tonelli and Pighin [2009] employs a machine learning framework to reach higher precision.

Linking Wordnets to Each Other While the focus of linking wordnets to other kinds of resources is to expand the coverage of lexical information types in one particular language, another important direction is to create links between wordnets in different languages. This is obviously useful for tasks such as cross-lingual information retrieval or machine translation, as the intention is to obtain LLKBs which provide high-quality expert knowledge about the respective languages.

One of the earliest attempts to bring together separate efforts to create wordnets across Europe was *EuroWordNet* [Jansen, 2004, Vossen, 1998]. *BalkaNet* [Stamou et al., 2002] is a closely associated project which aimed at adding wordnets for Bulgarian, Greek, Romanian, Serbian, Turkish, and Czech. The *Meaning Multilingual Central Repository* (MCR) [Atserias et al., 2004] does the same for Spanish, Catalan, Basque and Galician. While the *EuroWordNet* project has long ended, many insights and developments made in this project are still relevant, for instance the so-called *Interlingual Indexes* (ILI) which connect concepts in different languages. The *MultiWordNet* [Pianta et al., 2002] project has very similar goals, but a different approach—here, the idea is not to align existing separate wordnets, but rather to use the English WordNet (which is the most elaborate among them) as "blueprint" for creating wordnets in other languages. A similar endeavor was undertaken in the *Universal WordNet* project [De Melo and Weikum, 2008, 2009, 2010], which (as mentioned above) also includes links to Wikipedia.

2.4 MANUAL AND COLLABORATIVE LINKING

To cope with the task of fully linking two resources, most work has been focused on doing this automatically, or at least semi-automatically to reduce the manual work load. While we have discussed many of these efforts in this chapter, the most straightforward way to create linked resources is still to identify equivalent senses manually. To guarantee a high level of quality, two basic options exist: either the linking is performed by a closed group of experts, or by a large group of collaborators in an open process.

One of the most prominent projects for expert-based linking of resources is *SemLink* [Bonial et al., 2013, Palmer, 2009]. It includes a manual linking between the verb senses of PropBank and VerbNet classes, and between VerbNet classes and FrameNet frames. In addition, there are verb sense-specific mappings between the semantic roles of VerbNet, FrameNet, and PropBank.

The collaborative approach to linking is used in Wiktionary, OmegaWiki, and Wikipedia. However, this is not a systematic process—the main focus of each community is clearly to improve and extend the content of the respective resource. Thus, the linking is usually considered optional "icing" to provide additional background information on a particular concept, and not essential information. For instance, for OmegaWiki only a few thousand links to Wikipedia exist [Matuschek, 2014], which is still far from a complete alignment. It would, however, be no big issue to complete these links in collaborative resources considering the size of the workforce— ironically, the small set of editors is exactly the perennial challenge for the linking of expert-built resources, even more so as usually a linking is desired which is as complete as possible. One of the earliest projects trying to achieve this is *Cyc* [Reed and Lenat, 2002], an ontology project established in the 1980s with the goal of representing everyday common sense knowledge as accurately as possible, and which is comparable to YAGO. Hence, several smaller and specialized ontologies are included, but also general-language resources like WordNet. It is still under development, and apart from the commercial version there is also a freely available one.

Recently, manual effort is mostly used for creating evaluation or training datasets, while most of the actual linking work is done automatically using one of the more and more sophisticated algorithms for sense linking. We will discuss these linking algorithms in the next chapter.

2.5 CHAPTER CONCLUSION

We gave a high-level and broad overview of previous work on constructing LLKBs and organized it in a way that highlights a number of fundamental aspects:

- automatic vs. manual linking of LKBs: linking LKBs manually at scale requires a collaborative approach to linking rather than an expert-based one;

- intrinsic vs. task-based evaluation of the constructed LLKBs:

    - linking of LKBs with the primary goal of enhancing a particular NLP task: while this line of work always extrinsically evaluated the added value of combining LKBs, the linking task itself has often been greatly simplified: often, only selected information types relevant for the task at hand have been included in the combined LLKB;

    - linking of wordnets to other LKB types with the primary goal to study the linking task itself: while this line of work provided insights into the linking task, it often did not extrinsically evaluate the benefit of combining LKBs on an NLP task;

- the complementary nature of the LLKBs BabelNet and UBY: we pointed out that BabelNet and UBY, two large-scale approaches to linking LKBs, are complementary in many ways, which makes each of them suitable for different NLP tasks.

In conclusion, the survey in this chapter should provide a big picture of previous research on LLKB construction—in order to enable the interested reader to adequately position current research on this topic.

CHAPTER 3

Linking Algorithms

In the previous chapter we have introduced the notion of word sense linking (WSL) as the alignment of senses (or concepts) from different lexical-semantic resources, and we also presented several different projects which link resources at the word sense level for different purposes. While we also briefly covered manual construction approaches, we established that the most interesting ones in terms of flexibility and scalability are those which employ (semi-)automatic construction methods. In this chapter, we want to dive deeper into this topic and present different algorithmic approaches for identifying equivalent concepts across resources.

However, to better define the scope of this task and its peculiarities, we first want to take a step back and examine related problems from other fields. This will help in making it more clear what special problems arise when matching LKBs as opposed to, for instance, ontology matching or semantic relatedness calculation, and in what ways the corresponding algorithmic approaches can consequently be discriminated from related efforts. After this, we present the main evaluation metrics for WSL to help contextualize the approaches, and then discuss, in three distinct sections, three different angles from which this problem has been addressed: approaches based on the similarity of glosses of word senses, approaches based on the graph structure of LKBs, and a combination of both. As discussed in Chapter 1, glosses and semantic relations (inducing a structure) are the two ubiquitous ways to describe senses in different LKBs.

3.1 INFORMATION INTEGRATION

3.1.1 ONTOLOGY MATCHING

An ontology is formally defined as a specification of a conceptualization [Euzenat and Shvaiko, 2013]. In other words, it provides the vocabulary for describing a particular domain, and specifies the meaning of the terms used in this vocabulary. As a rule, well-defined relations between concepts such as *subclass* exist which add structure to the ontology and at the same time define the properties of its instantiations. For example, *car* is a subclass of *vehicle*, so if a vehicle can be used for transportation a car can trivially be used for this purpose as well. Such reasoning over ontologies is usually one of the desired properties, and one of the main reasons for applying them to real-world data analysis problems. Many LKBs can also be interpreted as ontologies as they contain corresponding relations between concepts [Veale et al., 2004]. However, unlike most ontologies, the LKBs we consider are not limited to a particular domain as they aim to encompass the entirety of real-world concepts and perceptions expressible via written language. Examples for such "language ontologies" are OmegaWiki (Section 1.2.3), OntoWiktionary [Meyer, 2013] or some of the resources contained in the Linguistic Linked Open Data Cloud.

The matching of ontologies is relevant if different conceptualizations need to be used in conjunction or merged. For instance if a company is merged with another one the internally used ontologies for the goods they produce must be harmonized. Hence, many different approaches have been developed, which are generally comparable to the ones suggested for WSL and can for most part be sorted into one of two broad categories.

- Terminological approaches are based on the lexical comparison of ontological entities and their descriptions [Cohen et al., 2003, Yatskevich and Giunchiglia, 2004].

- Structural approaches utilize the relationships between entities and try to find well-matching substructures in both ontologies [Giunchiglia et al., 2004, Maedche and Staab, 2002].

Hybrid approaches combining both directions seem to show the best results [Le et al., 2004]. The so-called extensional approaches present a vastly different paradigm which cannot straightforwardly be applied to WSL [Dhamankar et al., 2004, Doan et al., 2003]. These compare the actual instantiations of an ontology to identify entities which are similar and align the ontologies based on this. For example, it would be possible to look up the instances which are categorized as ANIMAL by one ontology and see if their attributes (like number of legs, size etc.) match the instances in the other ontologies. This is helpful in case of ontologies with very different descriptions or structures. Such an approach is not applicable to WSL, as there usually is no way to find out which real-world entities are covered by a specific word sense—e.g., it is not possible to look at all existing (or even hypothetic) cats and see if they are covered by a sense definition in Wiktionary.

On a related note, another interesting difference to WSL is that in an ontology different entities usually have very different attributes (such as the aforementioned attributes for an animal). This is a key feature for ontologies as they are tailored for specific domains and need to reflect the discriminating properties of heterogeneous objects. As such, the consideration of the number and properties of attributes is as important for ontology matching as the examination of their content. For LKBs, on the other hand, the description of the concepts is usually streamlined in the sense that the same set of descriptive features (such as gloss, example sentences etc.) is used for each concept. These features need thus be general enough to apply to all different kinds of concepts, while this is not a requirement for ontologies. Moreover, the well-defined semantics of relations, which are often utilized by ontology matching algorithms, are not always given in WSL. While there are, for instance, approaches which exploit particular relations in WordNet, these algorithms are not applicable to all LKBs. In Wikipedia, for example, links between articles usually represent only a general notion of relatedness without specifying its exact nature, and for FrameNet, the participation of senses in the same frame is a sign of relatedness which is hard to more specifically make statements about. To add to that problem, many resources, especially collaboratively constructed ones, suffer from disconnected or sparse graphs which makes the usage of structural approaches ineffective, at least in isolation.

In summary, ontology matching approaches are usually not well-suited for WSL, as the participating resources are usually only lightly structured, not as strictly specified from a semantic perspective, and instantiations of concepts are usually not available for examination. WSL algorithms (at least those which aim to be generally applicable) can only rely on the few semantic information types which are shared among many resources, such as glosses and example sentences, and the exploitation of structural information in terms of paths and distances, if no strict assumptions about the semantics of the relations are made.

3.1.2 DATABASE SCHEMA MATCHING

Database schema matching is, in many ways, comparable to ontology matching as the objects to be matched and the relations between them are strictly defined from a technical perspective, for instance, via foreign key relations which connect certain database tables. Thus, many approaches from ontology matching are also applicable in this case [Berlin and Motro, 2002]. The fundamental difference, however, is that in many cases a semantic interpretation of the database content is not explicitly given. While database schemata can also model real-world concepts and relations, there is often no other way to interpret the information than the tables' and attributes' names. Moreover, database relations by means of keys also express no more than a "relationship" between two tables in a generic, technical sense. Their actual interpretation is usually harder than for table attributes as most database system implementations such as SQL do not allow explicitly naming such relations.

Thus, even more than for ontology matching, algorithmic approaches for schema matching rely on technicalities such as number and data types of the attributes and instantiations of entities, i.e., extensional matching [Kang and Naughton, 2003]. Graph-based approaches are further hampered by the fact that different database design paradigms allow expressing the exact same information with a different segmentation and allocation of data across tables. Thus, in summary, this task is even further removed from WSL as semantic interpretation of the data for alignment purposes is less relevant than metadata- or instantiation-based algorithms.

3.1.3 GRAPH MATCHING

Another related problem, which by definition can only rely on structural properties, is graph matching, or more precisely, the detection of graph isomorphisms. The task is defined as calculating pairs of nodes from two distinct graphs which correspond to each other in the respective graph topologies. The challenge here is that, as with database schema matching, usually no additional information is given which allows the semantic interpretation of the graph structure. In general, the only information available is whether two nodes in a graph are linked or not, possibly with additional edge weights. Hence, without further constraints, an effort exponentially increasing with the number of nodes is necessary, rendering the task NP-hard [Arvind et al., 2012], but not NP-complete [Schöning, 1988].

For the application of graph isomorphism algorithms to WSL, it is possible to impose additional constraints such as limiting the set of candidates which are possible matches for a particular node. We would, however, still be facing the problem that LKB topologies are very different, as the interpretation and manifestation of edges between nodes (such as semantic relations) varies considerably and exact matches of subgraphs are thus not very likely. Consequently, for alignments of sufficient coverage and precision, less restrictive, heuristic matching seems necessary, in combination with gloss-based approaches which provide the necessary background knowledge to properly interpret the graph structure.

3.2   EVALUATION METRICS FOR WSL

The performance of a linking algorithm is usually assessed with a variety of different metrics, measured against gold standard datasets which were created by human annotators and are known to be correct. To calculate them, it is necessary to count the number of all possible decisions made: (i) true positives (TP), i.e., correct detection of positive examples, (ii) true negatives (TN), i.e., correct detection of negative examples (non-linkings), (iii) false positives (FP), i.e., examples which are linked but should not be, and (iv) false negatives (FN), i.e., examples which are not linked but should be.

Precision   reports how many of our decisions to link two senses are correct, i.e., the higher the precision of our algorithm the more confident we can be that the senses we link are equivalent. It is formally defined as:

$$P = \frac{TP}{TP + FP}.$$

Recall   reports how many of the positive examples in the gold standard are found by our algorithm, i.e., the higher the recall of our algorithm the more confident we can be that we detect all valid links between senses. It is formally defined as:

$$R = \frac{TP}{TP + FN}.$$

F-measure   (or F-score) is the harmonic mean of precision and recall. It is usually considered as the crucial linking metric, as neither precision nor recall are useful in isolation. They are also antagonistic: perfect precision can be achieved by not linking at all (no incorrect decision is made), while perfect recall is achieved by linking everything (no link is missed). F-measure is defined as:

$$F = \frac{2 \cdot P \cdot R}{P + R}.$$

Accuracy   reports how many of the decisions made by the algorithm are correct in total, i.e., considering both positive and negative examples. While this is also a valid indicator of linking quality, it should be carefully judged depending on the dataset. If the data is heavily skewed, good accuracy can easily be achieved by always assigning the majority class, e.g., if 90% of the gold standard examples are non-linkings, a baseline linking nothing would reach an accuracy of 0.90. Thus, F-measure usually reflects the quality of the alignment better. Accuracy is defined as:

$$A = \frac{TP + TN}{TP + TN + FP + FN}.$$

3.3   GLOSS SIMILARITY-BASED WSL

In this section, we would like to start the discussion of WSL approaches by examining similarity-based algorithms, as glosses are indispensable for humans to recognize the meaning of an encoded sense, and thus also a logical way of assessing the similarity of senses. For tasks such as WSD, the gloss can also be directly exploited, as one common approach is to compare this gloss to the context of a word to correctly disambiguate it [Lesk, 1986]. Thus, it seems natural that a wide variety of approaches for WSL are also based on gloss similarity.

In Section 2.3, we have already discussed several existing aligned resources and the motivation behind the respective projects. In order to avoid redundancy, we will not discuss them in detail again, but rather focus on presenting three of the most common similarity metrics for glosses; namely gloss word overlap, semantic relatedness expressed by semantic vectors, and Personalized PageRank (PPR) scores [Agirre and Soroa, 2009]. Table 3.1 gives an overview of the different similarity metrics used in the various LLKBs mentioned in Section 2.3.

3.3.1   WORD OVERLAP

The basic idea of word overlap measures has its roots in set theory, considering the words contained in glosses as members of sets whose similarity can be directly measured—for instance, by just comparing how many members are shared between the sets s_1 and s_2, and normalization over the set sizes. This notion is directly expressed by Simple Matching Coefficient (SMC):

$$SMC(s_1, s_2) = \frac{Number\ of\ matching\ words}{Total\ number\ of\ words}.$$

Two slightly more sophisticated measures, which are more commonly used in practice, are the Jaccard distance, defined as

$$J(s_1, s_2) = \frac{|s_1 \cup s_2| - |s_1 \cap s_2|}{|s_1 \cup s_2|}$$

and the Dice Coefficient:

$$D(s_1, s_2) = \frac{2|s_1 \cap s_2|}{|s_1| + |s_2|}.$$

However, as the Dice Coefficient does not satisfy the triangle inequality, it is not as straight-forwardly usable in practice.

Note that for these approaches to work effectively, a certain degree of preprocessing (tokenization, stopword removal, case normalization, etc.) is sensible in order to get more accurate results.

3.3.2   VECTOR REPRESENTATIONS

A more elaborate way to calculate similarity between texts, and thus specifically between glosses, is to represent them in a multi-dimensional vector space. The usual approach is to consider each word in a text as one dimension (again, preprocessed for improved accuracy), and then assign a weight to each dimension (this is generally called a bag of words, or BOW for short). The simplest option for weighting is to merely mark the presence or absences of a word (i.e., binary weights), however, this does not account for different word frequencies—the same is the case for the aforementioned overlap measures, which is why this option is generally disregarded. A better way is to use the counts of all words in the glosses as values, but it is more common to also normalize these in relation to the set of all glosses. A frequently used approach is the $tf * idf$ metric which tries to capture the importance of words in the whole corpus of documents D, by combining the term frequency $tf(t, d)$ of a term t within a single document d with the inverse document frequency, commonly defined as

$$idf(t, D) = log\frac{N}{\{d \in D : t \in D\}}.$$

A high value for $tf * idf$ is thus reached by a high term frequency in the given document and a low document frequency of the term in the whole corpus.

The second step after calculating the vectors is to compute the distance (or similarity) between them. A straightforward way to do so is the cos similarity. In the geometric interpretation of the vector space, the goal is to calculate the cosine of the angle between vector representations $V(s_1)$ and $V(s_2)$ of the two senses s_1 and s_2. It is defined as follows:

$$cos(s_1, s_2) = \frac{V(s_1) \cdot V(s_2)}{||V(s_1)|| \, ||V(s_2)||}.$$

While more complex measures are conceivable, the cos similarity has proven to be a robust and scalable solution for calculating text similarities. It is especially interesting for gloss similarities, as one of its major criticisms is the limited suitability for long documents—this issue does obviously not apply here.

3.3.3   PERSONALIZED PAGERANK

The Personalized PageRank (PPR) algorithm [Agirre and Soroa, 2009] also estimates the semantic relatedness between two word senses s_1 and s_2 by examining the glosses. However, it is sometimes argued that this is not strictly a text similarity measure, as the similarity score is calculated using a graph-based algorithm based on the original Google PageRank [Brin and Page,

1998]. More precisely, the glosses are represented as semantic vectors Pr_{s_1} and Pr_{s_2} where the main idea of choosing Pr is to identify those nodes in the graph that are central for describing a sense's meaning. These nodes should have a high centrality (that is, a high PageRank score), which is calculated as

$$Pr = c\, M\, Pr + (1 - c)\, v$$

with the damping factor c controlling the random walk, the transition matrix M of the underlying semantic graph, and the probabilistic vector v, whose i^{th} component v_i denotes the probability of randomly jumping to node i in the next iteration step. The formula is recursively defined as the algorithm starts out with random vectors and iterates toward the optimal solution by means of the transition matrix.

A popular variant for calculating the final PPR score is the one introduced by Niemann and Gurevych [2011]:

$$PPR(s_1, s_2) = 1 - \sum_i \frac{(Pr_{s_1,i} - Pr_{s_2,i})^2}{Pr_{s_1,i} + Pr_{s_2,i}}.$$

Unlike in the traditional PageRank algorithm, the components of the jump vector v are not uniformly distributed, but personalized to the sense s by choosing $v_i = \frac{1}{m}$ if at least one lexicalization of node i occurs in the definition of sense s, and $v_i = 0$, otherwise. The normalization factor m is set to the total number of nodes that share a word with the sense descriptions, which is required for obtaining a probabilistic vector.

To be able to apply such a graph-based algorithm, it is obviously necessary to have a semantic graph, i.e., one representing a network of concepts, as a foundation. In the original implementation by Agirre and Soroa [2009] the WordNet 3.0 graph is used as reference, but in later work PPR was extended to other graphs such as Wikipedia [Pilehvar and Navigli, 2014].

3.3.4   ADDITIONAL REMARKS

After the similarity scores are calculated, it is still necessary to make a decision based on them. The most straightforward way which has been discussed is to chose the candidate with the highest score (regardless of the absolute value) [Henrich et al., 2011]—however, this precludes the possibility of assigning several candidate senses to one source sense in case of differing sense granularities. Another way is to use a fixed similarity threshold [Pilehvar and Navigli, 2014] or learn an ideal threshold on a training set [Hartmann and Gurevych, 2013, Meyer and Gurevych, 2011, Niemann and Gurevych, 2011]. While the latter method reliably yields good results on various datasets, the additional effort of creating a sufficiently large training set should not be underestimated.

Another aspect which has been considered in the literature is the applicability to languages other than English. Word overlap measures and vector representations are inherently language independent, only the normalization and preprocessing need to be adapted, for instance to correctly capture frequencies in morphologically rich languages like German. For the PPR similarity,

Table 3.1: Approaches linking LKBs manually (top), using gloss overlap (middle) or some other notion of semantic relatedness (bottom)

Work	Method	Resource Pair
Reed and Lenat [2002]	manual	WordNet-Cyc
Shi and Mihalcea [2005]	manual/structure	WordNet-FrameNet
Mihalcea [2007]	manual	WordNet-Wikipedia
Suchanek et al. [2007]	overlap	WordNet-Wikipedia
Knight and Luk [1994]	overlap	WordNet-LDOCE
Kwong [1998]	overlap	WordNet-LDOCE/Roget
Burgun and Bodenreider [2001]	overlap	WordNet--UMLS
Ruiz-Casado et al. [2005]	overlap	WordNet-Wikipedia
De Melo and Weikum [2010]	overlap	WordNet-Wikipedia
Henrich et al. [2011]	overlap	GermaNet-Wiktionary
Navigli [2006]	relatedness	WordNet-ODE
Toral et al. [2009]	relatedness	WordNet-Wikipedia
Meyer and Gurevych [2011]	relatedness	WordNet-Wiktionary
Niemann and Gurevych [2011]	relatedness	WordNet-Wikipedia
Hartmann and Gurevych [2013]	relatedness	FrameNet-Wiktionary
Matuschek et al. [2013]	relatedness	Wiktionary-OmegaWiki
Gurevych et al. [2012a]	relatedness	WordNet-OmegaWiki

the case is a little more complicated, as for the calculation of the semantic vectors a richly linked LKB in the respective language is required—while, for instance, GermaNet might be suitable for German, for many less-resourced languages the usage of this measure might be problematic.

An important issue in this context is the cross-lingual linking of senses, i.e., the linking of LKBs in different languages. For this particular task, it was shown that reducing the problem to the monolingual case using a state-of-the-art machine translation engine on one of the resources yields satisfactory results [Gurevych et al., 2012a]. Other works such as Spohr et al. [2011] suggest using a third pivot languages to facilitate the mapping.

In general, similarity-based approaches give reasonable results (with precision usually in the range of 0.60-0.80), but they suffer from the inherent problem that they depend on the formulation the glosses, which might lead to problems in case of insufficient lexical overlap (known as the "lexical gap"; see for instance Meyer and Gurevych [2011]). Consider these two senses of *Thessalonian* in Wiktionary and WordNet : "A native or inhabitant of Thessalonica" and "Someone or something from, or pertaining to, Thessaloniki." These are (mostly) identical and should intuitively be linked, but there is no word overlap due to the usage of the synonyms *Thessalonica* and *Thessaloniki*. Nevertheless, this approach to WSL is not only intuitively reasonable, but also the method of choice for the first investigations in this area, thus representing the state of the art for a considerable time.

3.4   GRAPH STRUCTURE-BASED WSL

As we have seen in the previous section, linking based on gloss similarity is an intuitively valid approach which, in general, gives results significantly outperforming naive baselines. Nevertheless, we have also discussed that it suffers from the inherent problem of low recall if the glosses do not match lexically.

This difference between human judgment and similarity-based approaches for judging the equivalence of senses motivated the investigation of similarity measures which do not focus on the textual descriptions of senses, but the structure of the resources. This development is fueled by the recent emergence of electronic and especially machine-readable LKBs which allow automatic analysis and exploitation of their structure. In classic dictionaries, there are also references to related words, synonyms, etc., but these references are either not disambiguated at all, or additional look-up effort is required to induce a graph structure (cf. Engelberg and Lemnitzer [2001, Ch. 4.4]).

This situation is different for resources such as WordNet, which unambiguously connects synsets via semantic relations, or Wikipedia, which contains many hyperlinks between distinct articles, i.e., concepts. In both cases, a graph structure is implied, and it intuitively makes sense that directly connected concepts must be somehow related, while concepts which are in close proximity to each other probably belong to the same topic. This intuition was, for instance, confirmed in the context of the semantic relatedness task [Navigli and Ponzetto, 2012c, Rada et al., 1989, Zesch et al., 2008a], where the length of paths in the graph representation of a LKB turned out to be a good indicative feature. Following this idea, considering the structure of LKBs for WSL is a promising approach to alleviate the disadvantages of the similarity-based approaches, as the approaches do not depend on the properties of the glosses. Especially for expert-built resources and Wikipedia, a dense graph can be obtained which covers the majority of senses, while the graphs for the other collaboratively constructed resources have fewer edges in general [Garoufi et al., 2008, Matuschek, 2014].

A general issue with these graphs is that, although relations can carry certain explicit semantics (such as hyponymy), this is not guaranteed (e.g., for Wikipedia links), and different resources also express different aspects of relatedness (such as frames in FrameNet) which are not straightforwardly applicable to other resources. Thus, the most common approach for investigating algorithms based on the structure of multiple LKBs is to treat the edges as unlabeled. This is the most reasonable way to keep approaches flexible and generally usable, but this limits the potential benefit from exploiting the structure. Reasoning over relations is, for instance, used for many ontology matching approaches (see Section 3.1.1), and also for WSL many approaches have been suggested which make explicit use of the semantics encoded in the relation. Table 3.2 gives an overview of the approaches discussed in this section.

3.4.1   WIKIPEDIA CATEGORY ALIGNMENT

Toral et al. [2008] align WordNet synsets to Wikipedia categories by comparing and matching the WordNet tree structure to the Wikipedia category graph. They reach very good results, with an F-measure of up to 0.82 depending on the configuration. Their approach is, however, not applicable to the general case of WSL for several reasons. First, they only focus on matching Wikipedia concepts with compatible "instance of" relations in WordNet, i.e., abstract concepts which have real-world instantiations (e.g., "Tom Cruise" is an instance of "actor"). Concepts which do not adhere to this pattern are disregarded. This is valid in the scope of the particular case, but it does not cover the general case and is especially ill-suited for other parts of speech since, for instance, verbs cannot be instantiated.

Ponzetto and Navigli [2009] also propose a graph-based method to tackle the problem of aligning WordNet synsets and Wikipedia categories, with the purpose of restructuring the Wikipedia category graph in a subsequent step. Using semantic relations, they build WordNet subgraphs for each Wikipedia category and then align those synsets which are the best topological match according to these subgraphs, reaching an accuracy of 0.81. Like Toral et al. [2008], they only focus on a particular kind of semantic relation in WordNet ("is a" relations, expressing hyperynymy) in order to cover their specific application scenario, which is not directly applicable to parts of speech other than nouns. Moreover, the potentially useful information in the category graph is disregarded in the alignment step as only the WordNet taxonomy is used as an information source for linking.

3.4.2   SHORTEST PATHS

Laparra et al. [2010] present the SSI-Dijkstra+ algorithm, which is based on calculating shortest paths, to link FrameNet lexical units (LUs, the FrameNet equivalent to word senses) to WordNet synsets and create the combined resource *WordFrameNet*. The basic idea is to align monosemous LUs first and, based on this, find the closest synset in the WordNet graph for the other LUs in the same frame. They reach a result of 0.79 (F-measure), however, they make some assumptions which apply only to their particular case. For instance, the algorithm not only relies on the semantic relations found in WordNet, but also from the enriched *eXtended WordNet* [Mihalcea and Moldovan, 2001a] in order to find a sufficient number of targets. Thus, it is not straightforwardly applicable to other resources which have no or only few relations such as Wiktionary and for which no such high-quality extensions exist. Moreover, for the case that no monosemous LU exists in a frame, they align to the most frequent sense. This information is not available in most other resources. The issue of missing monosemous "anchors" into WordNet could be tackled by also considering LUs from other frames connected via frame relations, i.e., exploiting the graph structure for FrameNet as well. However, as SSI-Dijkstra+ is originally a word sense disambiguation (not linking) algorithm, it disregards this structure and merely considers LUs as texts which are to be disambiguated in isolation. In other words, only the "local" information for each LU is used.

Navigli [2009a] aims at disambiguating WordNet glosses, i.e., assigning the correct senses to all non-stopwords of each WordNet gloss. His approach is to find the shortest possible circles in the WordNet relation graph to identify the correct disambiguation. This "resource-internal" WSD was in later work extended to the disambiguation of translations in the *Ragazzini-Biagi English-Italian bilingual dictionary* (RBEID) [Flati and Navigli, 2012], which is just a different formulation of the WSL of two LKBs, as the English and Italian part of the dictionary can be considered separate LKBs. They reach an F-measure of 0.85, nevertheless, the algorithm benefits from the circumstances of the task: i) the English and Italian parts of the RBEID have comparably dense graph structures, which is not always given in the general case, and ii) as the English and Italian entries were created in a coordinated effort, we can assume that most senses in one part are represented in the other (i.e., there is a high conceptual overlap), and also that the sense granularities are similar. Both of these properties make the task substantially easier than aligning two heterogeneous LKBs. Additionally, for the cross-lingual case, the identification of possible alignment candidates is usually also a separate issue, which, for instance, can be addressed by machine translation (see also Section 3.3.4). Here, the alignment candidates are already given by the list of translations for each entry.

Matuschek and Gurevych [2013] present Dijkstra-WSA, an algorithm which was designed in the context of the unified resource UBY. One of the design goals is to make the algorithm flexibly applicable to as many resources as possible. It is the first attempt to apply a graph-based algorithm to full graph representations of two arbitrary resources, not just sub-graphs. Akin to the approach by Laparra et al. [2010], the first step is to align trivial cases, i.e., those senses with the same lexeme and only one sense in either resource. For the remaining senses, these trivial alignments serve as bridges between the LKBs to compute the shortest path to each candidate sense with Dijkstra's shortest path algorithm [Dijkstra, 1959]. The candidate with the shortest distance is then assigned as the alignment target. An alternative is to define a fixed threshold for the maximum path length to allow 1:n alignments. A major downside of this algorithm is its dependence on a dense graph structure, which is why it struggles on sparse resources like Wiktionary. For this case, the authors suggested a two-step approach of using Dijkstra-WSA first and then catering for the unaligned senses with conventional gloss-based measures, which yielded satisfactory results.

3.5   JOINT MODELING

We have seen in the last two sections that similarity-based and structure-based approaches to WSA both have their advantages when covering different aspects of sense similarity, and these complement each other: the former approaches work generally well, but they struggle if the for-

Table 3.2: WSL works using the structure of LKBs

Work	Resource
Toral et al. [2008]	WordNet-Wikipedia categories
Ponzetto and Navigli [2009]	WordNet-Wikipedia categories
Laparra et al. [2010]	WordNet-FrameNet
Navigli [2009a]	Disambiguatoin of WordNet glosses
Flati and Navigli [2012]	RBEID (English part-Italian part)
Matuschek and Gurevych [2013]	Several (UBY)

mulation of glosses is too different. The latter approaches can cope with that, but are limited in their performance in case of sparse LKBs such as Wiktionary.

We already discussed the simple fallback approach by Matuschek and Gurevych [2013] which applies both ideas in two distinct steps. However, a logical next step is to combine these two perspectives into a joint framework. Usually, these more complex approaches rely on machine learning and appropriate feature engineering, some of them focusing on WordNet-specific information types, others taking a broader perspective. A general characteristic of these approaches is their dependency on manually annotated training data, which was not the case for the similarity metrics presented earlier.

3.5.1 MACHINE LEARNING APPROACHES

Ferrandez et al. [2010] align FrameNet LUs and WordNet synsets. For a candidate pair, they first traverse the relations in both resources independently to construct "neighborhood graphs," with the source word sense at the center. Then, for each neighbor (appearing in any or in both neighborhoods) they calculate the distance to the centering word of each neighborhood and produce a normalized similarity score based on this, hence incorporating structural information from both resources. Plainly spoken, if both senses have similar neighbors in the respective LKBs, they are also considered to be similar; this idea is in line with other graph-based approaches presented earlier. As an additional feature, they also consider the textual similarity between glosses, but only on the character level. Using 100 examples for training their classifier, they achieve an accuracy of 0.77. The algorithm heavily relies on the particular relation types in WordNet (e.g., hyponymy, meronymy) and FrameNet (e.g., inheritance, causative) to assign optimal edge weights for the graph, which impairs the applicability to other LKBs. Moreover, Ferrandez et al. [2010] do not investigate the behavior of their classifier in cases where either distances or gloss similarities are (partially) missing, as these cases are negligible when examining the expert-built resources FrameNet and WordNet. For collaboratively constructed resources such as Wiktionary, however, this possibility also needs to be considered.

Matuschek and Gurevych [2014] combine their original Dijkstra-WSA algorithm [Matuschek and Gurevych, 2013] with gloss similarity features. More precisely, they use cos and PPR similarity, along with the distances between senses calculated with Dijkstra-WSA, in different machine learning configurations from the WEKA toolkit [Hall et al., 2009] to achieve substantial improvements over their previous work in most cases. Although they experiment with other, more complex features, no significant improvement over this straightforward combination of glosses and structure can be achieved, which suggests that this small set of features works reasonably well for most resources. An additional insight is that Bayesian networks show the most robust performance across datasets, while at the same time showing a very good runtime efficiency, which was an important design goal for constructing the large-scale linkings in the context.

De Melo and Weikum [2008] also use a machine learning approach, not with the goal of aligning existing LKBs, but the closely related one of creating new ones. In particular, they aim to create wordnets in a target language L_0 other than English by using the structure of the Princeton WordNet as a "blueprint." They tackle this issue by first providing a set of candidate translations for the lexemes contained in a WordNet synset from translation dictionaries, and then deciding for each translation if it is appropriate for this synset or not, based on a manually annotated training set. They train the classifier on a large variety of features based on the structure and the content of WordNet, and thereby reach a precision of 0.81. However, this approach is not easily generalizable as they also use WordNet-specific features such as corpus frequencies which are not readily available for most LKBs. Moreover, the task is inherently easier than full-scale (cross-lingual) WSL, because deciding if a lexeme l is a valid lexicalization for a concept in WordNet and then *creating* a new corresponding synset in L_0 circumvents the more challenging step of *choosing* the correct target in an existing LKB.

3.5.2   UNSUPERVISED APPROACHES

Bond and Foster [2013] link wordnets in many different languages to Wiktionary in the course of the *Open Multilingual Wordnet* project. Their core alignment algorithm is based on gloss similarity (following Niemann and Gurevych [2011], see Section 3.3), but they also incorporate structural information by considering translation links, i.e., two senses are assumed to be equivalent if they share many translations. They use manually set thresholds to avoid creating training sets for each language, and while the accuracy is sufficient (around 0.90), a major issue is the relatively low coverage of translations in Wiktionary, especially for smaller languages, which impairs the recall of this approach. Also, although Bond and Foster [2013] briefly describe the relational structure of the various wordnets, they do not make use of any additional structural features for the actual alignment.

Building on their own previous work on Wikipedia categories [Ponzetto and Navigli, 2009], Navigli and Ponzetto [2012a] align WordNet with Wikipedia articles in the context of *BabelNet*, reaching an F-measure of 0.78 on their own gold standard data set. Besides using bag-of-words overlap to compute gloss similarity, they build "disambiguation contexts" for Wikipedia articles by, for instance, using redirect links, and then assigning word senses to the lexemes in these contexts. To achieve this, a graph structure is built from WordNet semantic relations covering all possible WordNet senses of all lexemes contained in such a context, and local proximity is used to make the alignment decision. However, the information contained in the graph structure of Wikipedia is not fully considered, as only a subset of Wikipedia links is used to compose the disambiguation contexts. Moreover, for the actual alignment step, just a locally restricted subset of WordNet relations is used to make the decision, not the full WordNet graph, which would potentially provide additional valuable information about the senses to be aligned.

In the context of BabelNet, Pilehvar and Navigli [2014] achieve good results by using a gloss similarity component (as described earlier) in conjunction with a novel graph-based approach. They adapt the already discussed PPR measure to operate on custom graph representations for several LKBs such as Wiktionary and Wikipedia. In this context, they also present new approaches for ontologizing and enriching these resources with further links, which is crucial especially for Wiktionary as it does not provide links between senses. Instead of then directly using the PPR similarity as feature for the linking, for each sense they separately identify the central nodes in either graph, restrict the graph to the monosemous ones and then calculate a ranking-based score on the intersection of both graphs. In this way, they obtain the best results for WSL which have been reported so far, without the need to resort to manually annotated training data as they use predefined similarity thresholds.

Table 3.3: Approaches to WSL using combined features

Work	Resource (pair)
Bond and Foster [2013]	WordNet-Wikipedia
Navigli and Ponzetto [2012a]	WordNet-Wikipedia
Ferrandez et al. [2010]	WordNet-FrameNet
De Melo and Weikum [2008]	WordNet construction
Matuschek and Gurevych [2014]	Several (UBY)
Pilehvar and Navigli [2014]	Several (BabelNet)

3.6   CHAPTER CONCLUSION

In this chapter, we discussed a variety of algorithms for linking of LKBs, and highlighted their particular strengths and weaknesses. We also covered the cross-lingual linking of LKBs which can be reduced to the monolingual case using state-of-the-art machine translation. It has become clear that the most important question to consider when choosing an algorithm is evaluating the available information in the resources to be linked. For instance, for unstructured (or "flat") textual resources, measures like cos or vector space similarity yield satisfactory, but not in all cases stellar results. If structural information, e.g., semantic relations, is available, graph-based approaches have shown promising results, but only if the structure is sufficiently elaborate, as is the case for Wikipedia or WordNet.

The most recent trend (and current state-of-the-art) shows that the combination of both structural and textual features is most promising, as these two directions complement each other's strengths and weaknesses nicely. This is especially true if manually annotated training data can be used to inform machine learning classifiers, but also in cases where this data is not available or the effort of creating it would be too high, good results can be achieved by manually setting similarity or distance thresholds.

Nevertheless, we have seen that this field of research evolved rather quickly, and new approaches and features for other resource combinations and languages will no doubt emerge quickly. Also ideas from other related areas such as ontology matching or schema matching (which we have also briefly discussed) will be examined more closely, and could lead to even better results in the future.

CHAPTER 4

Fundamental Disambiguation Methods

In this chapter, we introduce the task of "disambiguating textual units" in a broader sense that covers not only WSD, but also entity linking or Semantic Role Labeling (SRL). We will build upon this definition in this and also in the next chapter. The main part of this chapter presents fundamental methods addressing the task of disambiguating textual units and discusses how the performance of these methods has been enhanced by employing LLKBs. We conclude by pointing out the impact of LLKBs on sense-annotated corpora, which are important resources in the context of automatic disambiguation.

4.1 DISAMBIGUATING TEXTUAL UNITS

We start by introducing a set of related tasks that have a disambiguation step in common, i.e., textual units are disambiguated relative to a sense inventory. First, we define the notion of *textual unit*, and then the task of *disambiguating textual units*.

Definition <u>Textual Unit:</u>   We define a *textual unit* as the occurrence of a word, a multiword expression, including named entities, or a predicate-argument structure in text.

In contrast to words and multiword expressions, named entities can also occur only partially. For example, the multiword expression *sushi bar* (e.g., as in: *She went into a sushi bar*) completely changes its meaning if one of the parts are omitted (e.g., *She went into a bar*), or even becomes ungrammatical (e.g., **She went into a sushi*). Named entities, on the other hand, can usually occur just partially, e.g., *Tony Blair* can stand for the full named entity *Prime Minister Tony Blair*.

A word-level textual unit corresponds to a token, and a multi-word-level textual unit to a phrase, which might be discontinuous as in: *She <u>took</u> her car <u>in</u> for maintenance* where the predicate *take in* is discontinuous.

A predicate-argument-level textual unit corresponds to a (possibly discontinuous) phrase as well, consisting of the predicate word and its argument phrases. The following example illustrates the occurrence of a predicate-argument-level textual unit within a sentence ("arg" stands for "argument"): *Someday <u>he</u>[arg_1] will <u>recognize</u>[pred] <u>what he witnessed here</u>[arg_2]* .

Definition <u>Disambiguating Textual Units:</u>   The task of disambiguating textual units is to *manually or automatically* annotate them with sense identifiers from a particular sense inventory given in a LKB. This requires determining the meaning of textual units given their context, relative to a given set of senses.

Depending on the type of textual units to be disambiguated and on the particular sense inventory used, several variants of disambiguating textual units are commonly distinguished (the sense inventory is typically given by a LKB).

- WSD [Navigli, 2009b] considers the disambiguation of words or multiword expressions relative to a LKB such as WordNet.

- Entity linking [Erbs et al., 2011] disambiguates named entities (i.e., multi-word-level textual units) relative to a KB rich in named entities (such as Wikipedia or Freebase).[1] The close similarity of WSD and entity linking has also been reflected in a recent SemEval shared task that combines WSD and entity linking.[2]

- Relation extraction disambiguates predicate-argument-level textual units that correspond to relation mentions, i.e., only focusing on predicates that express relations provided in a KB (e.g., the relation EducatedAt as in: *Stephen Hawking graduated from Oxford* where the predicate expressing the relation is underlined). Accordingly, predicates and their arguments are disambiguated relative to relationships and named entities provided in factual KBs such as Freebase.

- SRL disambiguates predicate-argument-level textual units relative to a LKB providing predicate-argument structure information, such as FrameNet or VerbNet. Commonly, this disambiguation task is performed in two steps: first, the disambiguation of the predicate (typically a verb); and second, the labeling of the (identified) arguments with semantic roles—which depends on the disambiguation result since semantic roles are often predicate-specific (see, e.g., examples in Section 1.1.2).

4.2   ENHANCED DISAMBIGUATION USING LLKBS

In this section, we describe the major approaches to disambiguation and how their performance has been enhanced by using LLKBs.

4.2.1   APPROACHES

Two main approaches to the automatic disambiguation of textual units relative to a sense inventory can be distinguished: first, knowledge-based approaches relying on a KB (or LKB) as primary knowledge source, and second, machine learning approaches using sense-annotated corpora as primary knowledge source. Both approaches use a LKB which defines the sense inventory.

---

[1]In contrast, co-reference resolution is the task to link named entities to other mentions (such as pronouns) in a given discourse; co-reference resolution can thus be performed without any KB.
[2]http://alt.qcri.org/semeval2015/task13/

Knowledge-based approaches make use of information from LKBs to tackle the disambiguation task. There are the two main classes of *Lesk-based algorithms* and *graph-based algorithms*.

Lesk-based Approaches   Lesk-based approaches compare the context of the target textual unit with each of its sense definitions in a LKB, and assign the sense which has the lexical overlap or the highest semantic relatedness with the context. Their name refers to the seminal work where this idea was formulated for the first time [Lesk, 1986].

Since its introduction, numerous variations of the Lesk algorithm have been developed, e.g., using adapted versions of the lexical overlap measure, or extending the sense definitions given in the LKB in order to increase the lexical overlap [Baldwin et al., 2010, Banerjee and Pedersen, 2002, Miller et al., 2012]. One particular way to increase the coverage of the Lesk-algorithm is to use a distributional thesaurus [Iida et al., 2008, Miller et al., 2012]. For example, Miller et al. [2012] represent a sense as a bag-of-words derived from the gloss, synonyms, and example sentences provided by the WordNet sense inventory. Additionally, for each content word found in this extended sense definition, a distributional thesaurus [Biemann and Riedl, 2013] is used to identify the top 100 most similar words in a corpus. Those top similar words are then added to the sense definition, and the Lesk-algorithm is applied to perform WSD. The idea is that the test sentences are likely to contain the words present in the corpus-based distributional thesaurus. This allows the Lesk-algorithm to find more overlaps and thus, increases WSD performance.

A drawback of most Lesk-based algorithms is that they do not account for word order. Such information is important for verb senses, as the syntactic behavior of a verb reflects aspects of its meaning.

Approaches assigning a sense based on semantic relatedness, on the other hand, compute the semantic relatedness between the target word and its context, and the senses in a LKB [Henrich and Hinrichs, 2012, Pedersen et al., 2005]. Extensions of this approach use optimization algorithms to jointly disambiguate the target word and the other words in its context [Cowie et al., 1992, Decadt et al., 2004].

Graph-based Approaches   Graph-based approaches to the disambiguation of textual units have also been investigated with great success, similar to word sense linking. These approaches exploit the structure of the KBs. One of the first was the SSI algorithm which uses sophisticated rules for exploiting certain kinds of semantic relations in WordNet [Navigli and Velardi, 2005]. Other resources like Wikipedia [Mihalcea, 2007, Mihalcea and Faruque, 2004] were also investigated, as were more complex algorithms like, for instance, PPR, an algorithm which we also discussed earlier in this book [Agirre and Soroa, 2009, Agirre et al., 2009b]. In general though, it turned out that these graph-based approaches require rich and sophisticated structures to be directly applicable, so that supervised approaches came more into focus to avoid the need for these.

Machine Learning Approaches   Regarding machine learning approaches, there are three main paradigms that have been applied to the task of WSD: supervised [Màrquez et al., 2006], unsupervised [Pedersen, 2006], and semi-supervised. In *supervised learning*, sense-annotated corpora are used as training data to learn a classifier that performs the disambiguation task.

Supervised systems rely on manually sense-annotated corpora which are typically expensive to create, and they tend to be biased toward the text domain(s) of the training corpus [Yuret, 2004].

In *semi-supervised learning*, large amounts of unlabeled data are combined with small labeled datasets. Some of the previous semi-supervised approaches to WSD considered bootstrapping where a supervised classifier and a small number of seed instances or patterns are employed to bootstrap learning [Fujita and Fujino, 2011, Mihalcea, 2004, Yarowsky, 1995]. Those methods, however, often suffer from low precision. A more recent variant of semi-supervised learning called *distant supervision* is introduced in detail in Chapter 5.2.

Unsupervised learning usually involves statistical clustering of word occurrences in an unlabeled corpus (i.e., without any given sense inventory), a task which is also called *word sense induction*. Such methods can use large amounts of data, but the induced word senses may be difficult to map to a sense inventory. As a result, unsupervised WSD systems are at a disadvantage if they need to disambiguate relative to an inventory that is supplied to the supervised systems by virtue of the training data. For this reason, unsupervised learning is usually not used for WSD (according to our definition in Section 4.1), but rather for word sense induction. For further information on word sense induction, the interested reader should take a look at the dedicated SemEval competitions for this task [Agirre and Soroa, 2007, Jürgens and Klapaftis, 2013, Manandhar et al., 2010].

4.2.2   OVERVIEW OF WORK IN THIS AREA

Our discussion of works where LLKBs have been used for improving the performance of automatic disambiguation (see overview in Table 4.1) follows the main approaches to disambiguation introduced above. While distant supervision as an instance of semi-supervised learning has successfully exploited LLKBs (see Section 5.2), we are not aware of any supervised approaches having improved the WSD performance using LLKBs.

Lesk-based Approaches   Since Lesk-based algorithms rely on the lexical overlap between the context of the target word and sense definitions, previous works have used LLKBs in order to extend the sense definitions. Ponzetto and Navigli [2010] align WordNet senses with Wikipedia articles to automatically extend sense definitions. They employ a Lesk-based algorithm and a graph-based algorithm to evaluate the impact on WSD. While their evaluation demonstrates that the use of a LLKB boosts the performance of knowledge-based WSD, it is restricted to nouns, since Wikipedia provides very few verb senses. Shi and Mihalcea [2005] describe a rule-based semantic parser that performs SRL and relies on a LLKB integrating FrameNet and VerbNet, also including a linking between VerbNet selectional preferences and WordNet synsets, as well as FrameNet semantic roles and VerbNet syntactic arguments. Flati and Navigli [2013] use heuristic rules on BabelNet to disambiguate nominal verb arguments.

Graph-based Approaches   In the area of graph-based approaches, the LLKB BabelNet has been used for a variety of different approaches to the disambiguation of textual units, also including entity linking and multilingual WSD [Moro et al., 2014b, Navigli and Ponzetto, 2012b,d]. Due to its rich graph structure, BabelNet lends itself particularly well to these algorithms. The approach by Moro et al. [2014b] tackles WSD and entity linking jointly and in a uniform way by leveraging a graph random walk algorithm for creating a graph structure of the text based on the BabelNet graph, and applying a densest subgraph heuristic for disambiguating the text. Agirre et al. [2014] present a method based on the Meaning Multilingual Central Repository (MCR), which is methodologically interesting due to its novel use of random walk algorithms.

Table 4.1: Disambiguating textual units using LLKBs

Work	KB	Task/Textual Unit
Ponzetto and Navigli [2010]	WordNet-Wikipedia	English WSD: nouns
Shi and Mihalcea [2005]	VerbNet-FrameNet	English SRL
Navigli and Ponzetto [2012d]	BabelNet	Multilingual WSD
Flati and Navigli [2013]	BabelNet	English WSD: verb arguments
Moro et al. [2014b]	BabelNet	Multilingual WSD, English entity linking
Agirre et al. [2014]	MCR	English WSD

Reflection   We have seen that the enriched sense representations available in LLKBs function as an enabler for well-performing rule-based approaches, such as Lesk-based algorithms. Similar as for the Lesk-based approaches, the combination of several LKBs provides the graph-based algorithms with richer sense representations in the form of a denser network of relations between senses. This directly leads to higher precision as well as recall due to the broader information base.

While both BabelNet and MCR can in principle be used for multilingual disambiguation, there are few multilingual evaluation datasets compared to English. For this reason, the majority of works listed in Table 4.1 have been evaluated for English.

4.3   ROBUST DISAMBIGUATION HEURISTICS

While the automatic disambiguation of corpus instances is a hard problem in general, especially when considering verbs and a fine-grained sense inventory such as WordNet, the situation is different when a LLKB such as UBY is used, which allows flexible movement between several sense inventories of different granularity. This flexibility can be exploited in specific semantic tasks where a heuristic disambiguation step using the fine-grained WordNet sense inventory can be combined with a mapping to a more coarse-grained sense inventory.

For example, Flekova and Gurevych [2015] used the LLKB UBY as a source of semantic features in the task of profiling fictional characters in books. They found semantic aspects of verbs to be effective for the classification of fictional characters into several psychologically motivated types. The particularly successful features for verbs were the (sense-specific) VerbNet classes. In order to extract these features, they employed a robust disambiguation heuristic which combines the most-frequent-sense heuristic using WordNet with the mapping to the more coarse-grained verb classes of VerbNet. Although WordNet's most-frequent-sense heuristic might yield an incorrect WordNet sense, the mapping of this fine-grained sense to a more coarse-grained inventory is able to correct the wrong disambiguation in many cases. Consider as an example the sentence *She announced the winner of the competition to an excited audience.* with the target word *announce* and the most frequent sense "make known; make an announcement" (according to SemCor). While "make known; make an announcement" is incorrect relative to the WordNet sense inventory— the correct WordNet sense being "give the names of"—it is linked to the VerbNet verb class announce_say-37.7-1, which is the same verb class that is also linked to the correct WordNet sense. The classification experiments by Flekova and Gurevych [2015] demonstrate the effectiveness of this robust disambiguation heuristic.

A similar, but simpler, way of exploiting this heuristic combines WordNet's most-frequent-sense with a mapping to the WordNet semantic fields. For example, there are four different senses of *promise* in WordNet 3.1, the most frequent one and two others belonging to the semantic field "communication," and only one sense (the least frequent) belonging to a different semantic field "stative."

It is important to point out that this flexibility of moving between different, but linked sense inventories is only offered by LLKBs such as UBY that keep the original LKBs intact, as opposed to, e.g., BabelNet.

4.4   SENSE CLUSTERING

The driving motivation behind all of the presented linking efforts is the fact that not every resource is equally well suited for each task, e.g., because of different lexical and sense coverage or different information types. We saw in Section 4.2 that for word sense disambiguation, a combination of resources instead of a single one has proven beneficial to the performance. A related issue is that the actual annotation of word senses usually uses only a single sense inventory, and in most cases this is an expert-built one.

4.4.1   METHOD

The Princeton WordNet [Fellbaum, 1998a] is the predominant sense inventory for English because of its free availability, its comprehensiveness, and its use in dozens of previous studies and datasets. For German, GermaNet [Hamp and Feldweg, 1997] is the reference resource for WSD, although systematic investigation of German WSD has only recently begun [Henrich and Hinrichs, 2012].

However, there is much evidence that suggests that the sense distinctions of such expert-built wordnets are too fine-grained—i.e., they are more subtle than what is typically necessary for real-world NLP applications, and sometimes even too subtle for human annotators to consistently distinguish. This point has been made specifically for WordNet [Ide and Wilks, 2006], but applies to other resources as well. This makes improving upon experimental results difficult, while at the same time the downstream benefits of improving WSD on these resources are often not clearly visible.

Much prior work has therefore been dedicated to decreasing the granularity of LKBs through (semi-)automatic sense clustering. In this section, we describe how WSL can contribute a solution to the granularity problem.

Definition <u>Word Sense Clustering</u>:   Word sense clustering is the process of (manually or automatically) identifying senses in a LKB which are similar to such a degree that they could be considered the same, variants of each other, or subsenses of the same broader sense. The purpose of this is to merge these senses (i.e., to define the set of clustered senses as a single new sense) in order to facilitate the usage of the sense inventory in applications which benefit from a lower degree of polysemy.

As an example, the two WordNet senses of *ruin*—"destroy completely; damage irreparably" and "reduce to ruins"—are very closely related and could be used interchangeably in many contexts.

The focus of attention for clustering has almost exclusively been the English WordNet, and it has been shown that such clustering significantly enhances human inter-annotator agreement [Palmer et al., 2007]. While it has been shown that automatic WSD performance [Snow et al., 2007] also benefits from clustering WordNet senses, it must be taken into account that the random sense baseline is improved as well. Furthermore, the benefit of coarser WSD has yet to be proved in downstream tasks.

4.4.2   OVERVIEW OF WORK IN THIS AREA

Merging fine-grained senses into coarser units has been a perennial topic in WSD. Past approaches have included using text- and metadata-based heuristics (definition text, domain tags, etc.) to derive similarity scores for sense pairs in electronic dictionaries [Chen and Chang, 1998, Dolan, 1994], exploiting wordnets' semantic hierarchies to group senses by proximity or common ancestry [Buitelaar, 2000, Ide, 2006, Mihalcea and Moldovan, 2001b, Peters et al., 1998, Tomuro, 2001], grouping senses which share translations into another language [Resnik and Yarowsky, 2000], using distributional similarity of senses across usage contexts [Agirre and Lopez de Lacalle, 2003, McCarthy, 2006], exploiting disagreements between human annotators of sense-tagged data [Chklovski and Mihalcea, 2003], heuristics mapping senses to learned semantic classes [Kohomban and Lee, 2005], and deep analysis of syntactic patterns and predicate-argument structures [Palmer et al., 2004, 2007].

While all of the approaches mentioned above consider the senses of particular LKBs in isolation, another way to produce such a clustering is WSL, which was introduced in Chapter 2. If it is not restricted to 1:1 linking (i.e., a sense may participate in more than one pair), it is possible that a sense s in one resource A is assigned to several senses $t_1, \ldots, t_n$ in another resource B. Assuming that all links are valid, this suggests that $s \in A$ is more coarse-grained and subsumes the other senses, which in turn can be considered as a sense cluster within B. For example, the aforementioned senses of *ruin* could both be linked to the Wiktionary sense "to destroy or make something no longer usable," which would result in their merging.

Navigli [2006] induces a sense mapping between WordNet and the *Oxford Dictionary of English* [Soanes and Stevenson, 2003] on the basis of lexical overlaps and semantic relationships between pairs of sense glosses. WordNet senses which align to the same *Oxford* sense are clustered together. Snow et al. [2007] and Bhagwani et al. [2013] extend Navigli's approach by training machine learning classifiers to decide whether two senses should be merged. They make use of a variety of features derived from WordNet as well as external sources, such as the aforementioned *Oxford*-WordNet mapping or the *OntoNotes* corpus [Pradhan et al., 2007]. While their method results in an improvement over the baseline, it does require a fair amount of annotated training data, and the features are largely tailored toward WordNet-specific information types (e.g., shared antonym relations for two senses). This makes the transferability to resources lacking this information non-trivial. Matuschek et al. [2014] take a more flexible approach and use their WSL algorithm Dijkstra-WSA [Matuschek and Gurevych, 2013] to create linking-based clusterings of WordNet and GermaNet against three different LKBs, Wiktionary, Wikipedia, and OmegaWiki. They investigate how the different properties of these resources influence the clusterings, particularly with respect to performance for different parts of speech.

Reflection   While it has been shown that clustering can be effective when only considering a single resource, the benefits of using LLKBs (or more precisely, the sense linkings contained therein) lie mostly in the increased flexibility. The sense alignment approaches which have been recently introduced allow to combine several sources of knowledge and their respective rationales concerning the sense granularities. In this way, it is possible to fine-tune the clusters depending on the configuration of the end task, and it has even proven to be effective to use different resource linkings for clustering different parts of speech [Matuschek et al., 2014]. Moreover, the linking based approach also allows for increased flexibility—while resource-internal clustering strategies are often heavily tailored toward a particular LKB, recent linking algorithms have been shown to be applicable to many different kinds of resources.

4.5   SENSE-ANNOTATED CORPORA

Sense-annotated corpora are important resources for automatic disambiguation methods, in particular as evaluation datasets, but also as training data for machine learning.

In a sense-annotated corpus, word occurrences have been manually annotated with sense identifiers from a particular sense inventory. This annotation task requires determining the meaning of word occurrences given their context, relative to a given set of senses. Many sense-annotated corpora have been created in the context of the SemEval shared task series.[3]

Two types of sense-annotated corpora are commonly distinguished: first, lexical sample corpora where only instances of a set of selected lemmas—the lexical sample—are sense-annotated, and second, all-words corpora where all instances of open-class words (i.e., nouns, verbs, adjectives and adverbs) are annotated.

Provided that an all-words sense-annotated corpus constitutes a sufficiently large[4] language sample, it is a valuable source of information on the frequency distribution of the senses from any particular sense inventory. Therefore, sense-annotated corpora also play an important role for training statistical models.

Previous corpus annotation projects typically focused on a single sense inventory for the annotation, usually for one very specific purpose. For example, the subcat frames listed in COM-LEX Syntax have been tagged in a corpus [Macleod et al., 1996] in order to gain information about the actual frequency of the individual subcat frames in written text. The SemCor corpus is annotated with the English WordNet [Snyder and Palmer, 2004], while WebCage is annotated with senses from GermaNet [Henrich et al., 2012]. The so-called FrameNet full text corpus[5] comprises whole documents that have been annotated with FrameNet frames, i.e., the frame-evoking word, as well as the frame elements realized in the text. For German, there is a corpus annotated according to frame semantics called SALSA [Burchardt et al., 2006].

However, also multilayer sense-annotated corpora offering sense-annotation with different sense inventories in parallel and at multiple layers have gained popularity.

Multilayer sense-annotated corpora go as far back as OntoNotes [Hovy et al., 2006, Pradhan et al., 2007] and SemLink (PropBank annotated with syntactic structure and with VerbNet and FrameNet senses) [Palmer, 2009]. Larger and more recent efforts include the Groningen Meaning Bank [Basile et al., 2012b] and MASC [Passonneau et al., 2012]. Only recently the sense inventory from the LLKB BabelNet was used to create a sense annotated corpus [Moro et al., 2014a, Navigli et al., 2013].

It is important to point out that the multilayer annotations of word senses relative to several sense inventories establish an indirect linking of the participating LKBs at the word sense level. This follows directly from the observation that annotating words in a corpus with their sense identifier in a LKB yields a linking between those word occurrences and the senses in the LKB. Thus, multilayer sense-annotated corpora link the participating LKBs via the annotated corpus instances.

---

[3]https://en.wikipedia.org/wiki/SemEval
[4]The required size of the text sample depends on the application.
[5]https://framenet.icsi.berkeley.edu/fndrupal/fulltextIndex

Although it is still an open question whether multilayer sense-annotated corpora will provide a significant benefit in any NLP task, the promising results in the related area of LLKBs merit and motivate further investigations.

4.6   CHAPTER CONCLUSION

This chapter discussed benefits of using LLKBs in textual unit disambiguation. There are two main advantages of using LLKBs.

- The combination of several LKBs as sources of knowledge enables the underlying algorithms to use richer sense representations, either consisting of aggregated textual information (such as sense examples or sense definitions), or of a denser network of relations between senses. This sense enrichment allows better informed automatic decisions about the relationships between the textual units and their senses in a given document, thus improving both the precision and the recall of automatic methods.

- Another benefit of using LLKBs for automatic disambiguation is the resulting sense-annotation of corpora at multiple layers according to different sense inventories. Such multilayer sense-annotated corpora might be promising language resources, as there are several projects which construct such corpora manually (see previous section).

Finally, we emphasized that there is no one-size-fits-all LLKB.

- Multilingual tasks (e.g., multilingual WSD) benefit from LLKBs rich in multilingual information, such as BabelNet or MCR.

- The flexible use of different sense inventories for the purpose of heuristic WSD and sense clustering is only possible with a LLKB that models the original LKBs as separate lexicons, such as UBY. This way, the sense links serve as connecting paths to move between different sense inventories.

CHAPTER 5

Advanced Disambiguation Methods

This chapter presents advanced methods to address the task of disambiguating textual units and discusses how their performance has been enhanced by employing LLKBs. First, we consider the machine learning paradigm of distant supervision to generate training data, and second, we discuss recent work in Deep Learning on continuous vector space models of KBs and LKBs. We start by introducing the task of *Automatic Knowledge Base Construction* (AKBC), because it is one of the core tasks considered both within distant supervision and vector space modeling of KBs.

5.1 AUTOMATIC KNOWLEDGE BASE CONSTRUCTION

The task of AKBC is to either create a KB from scratch or to extend an existing KB. We will take a closer look at the latter variant which addresses the ever-recurrent problem of any KB and LKB: insufficient coverage of entries or information types regarding a given text corpus or application. Specifically, the main limitation of all disambiguation approaches using a fixed sense inventory from a LKB is the possibly insufficient sense coverage of the LKB.

AKBC on the foundation of raw texts such as websites or other corpora is immediately connected to the task of disambiguating textual units: AKBC comprises the subtasks of detecting instances (also-called "mentions") of KB entries in raw text, disambiguating the instances relative to a label inventory given by the KB, and finally extending the KB by new information inferred from the disambiguated instances.

A typical example of AKBC is the extension of a fact KB by new facts extracted from linguistically preprocessed raw text. Facts in a KB are represented as triples, i.e., a binary relation and its two arguments (also-called "subject" or "left-hand side" and "object" or "right-hand side"). For instance, the triple *(Stephen Hawking, EducatedAt, Oxford)* encodes the relation EducatedAt which holds between the two arguments *Stephen Hawking* and *Oxford*. Assuming that this triple is missing in a fact KB, the AKBC approach would detect, for example, the sentence *Stephen Hawking graduated from Oxford* as a mention of the EducatedAt relation based on the presence of the two named entities *Stephen Hawking* and *Oxford*. These two entities would be disambiguated relative to the inventory of (named) entities in the fact KB, while the verb phrase graduated from would be disambiguated relative to the inventory of relations. Based on such a successful disambiguation step, a new fact would be inferred from the processed sentence and added to the KB. It is important to note that the mention detection and disambiguation step relies on linguistic preprocessing resulting in an enhancement of the raw text, i.e., adding features that allow a comparison with KB entries; in our example this would be at least tokenizing and named entity tagging.

The AKBC approach is very similar to Open Information Extraction (OIE) like *KnowItAll* [Banko et al., 2007] where the basic idea is to automatically extract natural language statements and transform them into structured knowledge. In contrast to AKBC, OIE does not necessarily perform any disambiguation of the extracted statements relative to a KB.

One large-scale AKBC project based on the OIE paradigm is NELL (Never Ending Language Learner [Mitchell et al., 2015]). NELL uses the Web as text source, and since its start in 2010 has accumulated a KB of approximately 89 million beliefs with varying levels of confidence in November 2014.

In projects like the *Google Knowledge Vault* [Dong et al., 2014], it was discovered that existing (lexical) KBs can provide invaluable hints for judging the quality of the extracted information in a supervised learning setup and hence drastically improve the performance. With the recent rise of large-scale LLKBs, it can be presumed that the broader and richer foundation of information will also be helpful for this particular task.

In the context of fact KBs (as opposed to lexical KBs), another common approach to AKBC is to link existing KBs in order to increase the overall coverage of facts—we have discussed approaches for information matching of this kind in Section 3.1, and of course the problem statement closely resembles that of sense linking between LKBs (Chapter 2). Past approaches to AKBC, which are most prevalent in context of the Semantic Web, have mostly another one instance-based matching (for instance, matching "DE" in one KB to "Germany" in the other), and only recently the need to consistently match the schemata was widely recognized. Consequently, relatively simple rule-based approaches represent the current state-of-the-art in this area [Galárraga et al., 2013], but it is likely that more sophisticated approaches from the domain of WSL will be adopted in the future.

5.2   DISTANT SUPERVISION

Distant supervision as a more recent paradigm in semi-supervised learning (i.e., learning from a combination of labeled and unlabeled data) aligns a typically large KB with text: KB entries are linked to textual units using a matching criterion. Based on this linking of text and KB, any label contained in the KB entry can be transferred to the textual unit. This way of automatic training data generation for machine learning is the primary goal of distant supervision.

5.2.1   METHOD

Figure 5.1 illustrates the general method of distant supervision which we will now introduce in detail.

Definition <u>Distant Supervision:</u>   Distant supervision is the process of automatically linking entries in a KB with textual units (considered as their instantiations) in a text corpus using a matching criterion (step (1) in Figure 5.1). Such a linking allows the transfer of KB labels to corpus instances (step (2) in Figure 5.1). For instance, using a LKB and sense IDs as labels, textual units can automatically be sense-annotated. The two main stages of distant supervision can be described as follows.

1. **Matching criterion**: based on an enrichment of the text corpus using linguistic preprocessing (e.g., POS tagging, lemmatization, dependency parsing, or named entity recognition), the enriched textual units are compared to KB entries using a matching criterion. Examples of matching criteria are the simple matching of named entities in the text and in the KB, or the more complex similarity of corpus sentences and sense examples in a LKB using a similarity metric and a similarity threshold that has been calibrated on a labeled development set. Sometimes corpus instances and KB entries are converted into a common representation format (e.g., Weston et al. [2013] used a vector representation) in order to better determine their similarity.

2. **Label transfer**: if the matching criterion is met, a label from the KB entry can be transferred to the textual unit. Examples of textual units that can be labeled in this way are sentences (label: relation name), verb instances (label: sense ID), or verb arguments (label: semantic role label). Since the result of the label transfer stage is usually a sparse (only few instances obtain a label) and noisy (the accuracy of the automatic labels is low) labeling, distant supervision relies on huge amounts of unlabeled data. For instance, for distantly supervised verb sense disambiguation, Cholakov et al. [2014] used about one billion words from the English ukWAC corpus [Baroni et al., 2009] (containing two billion words).

In summary, distant supervision requires a large-scale KB with good label coverage, huge amounts of unlabeled data, and possibly also a small amount of manually labeled data in order to calibrate the threshold of a similarity calculation.

When distant supervision is used for training data generation, there are two different setups to be distinguished:

- data generation from scratch where the automatically labeled data is the only training data and

- data augmentation where the automatically labeled data is used to augment a manually labeled dataset.

5.2.2   OVERVIEW OF WORK IN THIS AREA

Distant supervision has become popular for the task of relation extraction and most previous works on distant supervision have considered this task; see overview in Table 5.1.

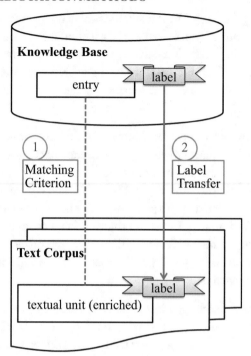

Figure 5.1: Method of distant supervision.

Mintz et al. [2009] (who introduced the term *distant supervision*) aligned text and KBs by recognizing named entities in text and linking them to the corresponding named entities in the KB. A similar approach had been introduced earlier by Bunescu and Mooney [2007] under the umbrella term "weak supervision;" they used a small amount of seed knowledge instead of a full KB to extract relations from text.

Most previous works on relation extraction employ the so-called "distant supervision assumption" which is specific for the task of relation extraction [Riedel et al., 2010]: "If two entities participate in a relation, *all sentences* that mention these two entities express that relation." Using this assumption for aligning text and KB leads to a certain amount of noise in the automatically labeled data. Consider as an example the relation Founded and the entities *Facebook* and *Mark Zuckerberg* participating in this relation. According to the matching criterion assumed by the distant supervision assumption, both sentences (1) and (2) below would be labeled as mentions of the relation *(Mark Zuckerberg, Founded, Facebook)*, although (2) clearly does not express this relation.

(1): *Mark Zuckerberg is co-founder and CEO of the social-networking website Facebook.*
(2): *Mark Zuckerberg is on Facebook.*

Follow-up research therefore developed various methods to reduce the noise created by using the distant supervision assumption for relation extraction. For example, Riedel et al. [2010] introduced the *modified* expressed-at-least-once assumption where not all sentences which mention the entities participating in particular relation are considered as relation mentions, but only a subset of at least one sentence; this modification leads to more accurate results. Hoffmann et al. [2011] and Surdeanu et al. [2012] cast the problem of relation extraction using the distant supervision assumption as a multi-label, multi-instance problem and suggest models that are specifically tailored toward this problem, and hence outperform previous related approaches.

Weston et al. [2013] use distant supervision to learn embeddings of relation mentions in text; their model learns a similarity function that scores the similarity of relation mention embeddings and relation embeddings learned from a KB.

Regarding LLKBs, BabelNet has been employed for the acquisition of relation patterns from text using distant supervision [Krause et al., 2012, Li et al., 2015, Moro et al., 2013]. They create an alignment of text and the LLKB BabelNet by means of disambiguating the text relative to the LLKB using Babelfy as the WSD algorithm. This alignment of text and LLKB is leveraged for the rule-based acquisition of relation patterns from text, which are then used for rule-based relation extraction.

Cholakov et al. [2014] present a new variant of distant supervision for the task of verb sense disambiguation, using the LLKB UBY. The alignment of text and UBY relies on the construction of a common, pattern-based representation format for corpus sentences and sentence level lexical information from UBY, such as sense examples and predicate argument structure information. Cholakov et al. [2014] experimentally evaluat the effect of varying the amount of sense links used to generate training data for WordNet WSD. They use the automatically labeled data to train WSD classifiers and their results demonstrate that increasing the amount of sense links improved the coverage of the training data and the performance of the WSD classifiers.

Hartmann et al. [2016] develop a distant supervision approach for SRL using UBY and SemLink as KBs. First, they generate sense-labeled data based on UBY, then they extend these to role-labeled data using SemLink. An evaluation on several FrameNet SRL datasets shows that their approach for training data generation is able to generalize across domains and languages.

Table 5.1 gives an overview of previous work on distant supervision according to the tasks considered.

Reflection   While distant supervision has become popular for the task of relation extraction— sometimes it is even used as a synonym for the "distant supervision assumption" in relation extraction—it is important to realize that the method of aligning a KB with text is much more general and can be used for a wide range of different tasks.

For other tasks than relation extraction, the type of KB and the matching criterion used are typically different. In particular, the type of knowledge a KB offers influences the choice of the matching criterion. For instance, we have seen that LKBs rich in sentence level lexical information, such as sense examples, can naturally be combined with a similarity metric.

Table 5.1: KBs used in distantly supervised approaches grouped by the task

Work	KB	Task
Mintz et al. [2009]	Freebase	English relation extraction
Riedel et al. [2010]	Freebase	English relation extraction
Hoffmann et al. [2011]	Freebase	English relation extraction
Surdeanu et al. [2012]	Freebase	English relation extraction
Weston et al. [2013]	Freebase	English relation extraction
Li et al. [2015]	Freebase, BabelNet	English relation extraction
Cholakov et al. [2014]	UBY	English WSD (verbs)
Hartmann et al. [2016]	UBY, SemLink	English and German SRL (verbs)

Cholakov et al. [2014] show that linked senses increase the overall percentage of text that could be automatically aligned with the KB, which is due to the enriched sense representations aggregating many different instantiations of the same lexical information; this higher variability increases the percentage of text instances that are similar to KB entries and thus improves the performance of a classifier trained on the automatically labeled text.

5.3 CONTINUOUS VECTOR SPACE MODELS OF KBS

Continuous vector space models of *knowledge bases* moved into the focus of research in the context of learning low-dimensional dense vector representations of words from large amounts of text [Bengio et al., 2003, Levy et al., 2015, Mikolov et al., 2013, Pennington et al., 2014], which are also-called *word embeddings*. Such word embeddings capture semantic and syntactic properties of words, i.e., the word embeddings of semantically or syntactically similar words are also close to each other in the vector space. They were originally developed as a neural language model [Bengio et al., 2003], for which a more efficient and nowadays widely used computation method—known as *word2vec*—was developed by Tomas Mikolov [Mikolov et al., 2013]. Levy and Goldberg [2014] showed that one variant of word2vec (skip-gram with negative-sampling) is implicitly factorizing a particular variant of the word-context matrix, which is well known from traditional vector representations of text as described in Section 3.3.2.

Similar to word embeddings which are trained on text, Vector Space Models (VSMs) of KBs (also-called *KB embeddings* or *structured embeddings*) are learned from large KBs and yield distributed representations of the textual units (e.g., words or phrases) present in a KB. KB embeddings have mainly been used in the context of distantly supervised relation extraction for *automatic knowledge base completion*, a task closely related to AKBC. Apart from this particular task, KB embeddings can be used as features in machine learning instead of or in addition to word or phrase embeddings learned from text, e.g., in deep neural networks.

5.3.1 METHOD

KB embeddings map the knowledge present in a KB to a low-dimensional vector space. In contrast to the traditional vector representation introduced in Section 3.3.2, which is sparse and high-dimensional, KB embeddings are dense vectors with a low dimension, e.g., ranging from 50 to several hundred. Depending on the kind of knowledge that is provided in a KB and that is to be captured by the VSM, different variants of VSMs have been developed.

Definition Continuous Vector Space Model of KB: Most VSMs of KBs model a KB as consisting of a *set of entities* and a *set of relations* between them. Entities might be concepts in an ontology (e.g., *Mark Zuckerberg, Facebook*) or word senses in a LKB (e.g., *tree, oak*), relations might be either ontological relations (e.g., *Founded*) or sense relations, such as hyponymy (e.g., *oak* is a hyponym of *tree*). Two entities e_1, e_2 related via a relation r form a relation triple (e_1, r, e_2). The set of relation triples constitutes a *knowledge graph* where nodes are entities and edges are relations between them. The knowledge graph model of KBs matches not only fact databases, but also LKBs, since the word senses can be viewed as entities related by sense relations or other relations.

KB embeddings are learned from large KBs using a similar training regime as in algorithms for learning word embeddings from text: the overall training objective is to arrive at a vector representation where vectors for entities that are close in the knowledge graph are also close in the vector space. For training, existing triples in the knowledge graph are considered as positive examples, and random samples of the non-existing triples of entities and relations as negative examples.

5.3.2 OVERVIEW OF WORK IN THIS AREA

Previous research has developed a large variety of VSMs for learning embeddings of triples representing facts. Therefore, we start by summarizing models that consider fact KBs, also including KB embeddings that are jointly learned from text and from KBs. Then, we discuss VSMs that specifically consider LKBs, such as WordNet.

Fact KBs Embeddings of fact KBs have mostly been developed for the purpose of KB completion (a subtask of AKBC), in particular, for adding new relations between entities by leveraging existing relations between entities in the KB. Most previous works in this area have performed their experiments on Freebase, some also used the subset of WordNet consisting of noun senses. For the experimental evaluation of the KB embeddings, the task of link prediction (i.e., relation prediction) is prevailing, but entity prediction and triple classification are sometimes performed as well. An overview is given in Table 5.2.

Guo et al. [2015] provide a review of previous approaches to learning KB embeddings and identify several commonalities with and differences to previous approaches. In order to represent relation triples, previous VSMs of KBs consider entity embeddings, as well as relation embeddings; relations are represented as operators in the vector space, taking the entity embeddings as arguments. There are differences regarding the definition of the relation operator: it can be formalized as a matrix [Bordes et al., 2011], a vector [Bordes et al., 2013], or a tensor [Socher et al., 2013].

Yang et al. [2015] introduce a generalized model that unifies previous multirelational embedding models by Bordes et al. [2013] and Socher et al. [2013] under a common framework. They evaluate their model using WordNet and Freebase on the link prediction task. The KB embedding presented by Guo et al. [2015] additionally includes a notion of semantic smoothness which exploits the semantic category of entities, i.e., entities having the same semantic category are close in the embedding space. Ji et al. [2015] develop an embedding model that uses two vectors for each entity and relation, one represents the meaning of an entity or a relation, the other vector is used to construct a mapping matrix for each entity-relation pair which represents a relation-aware projection of entities into the relation space.

More recently, various works have introduced models that learn relation paths, rather than only direct relations between entities. Guu et al. [2015] introduce a compositional training objective that improves the modeling of relations paths and can be applied to the class of composable VSMs of KBs, including, e.g., the TransE model by Bordes et al. [2013]. In their experiments, they use WordNet and Freebase and evaluate on path query answering and knowledge base completion. Neelakantan et al. [2015] use a recurrent neural network to construct vector representations for sequences of relations of any length, and thus are also able to predict new relations paths. Luo et al. [2015] present a model that explicitly models relation paths of length two, i.e., paths that share a common bridging entity.

Fact KBs and Text   Another line of research in VSMs for KB completion also takes into account text as a source of new relations that can be added to the KB. This is motivated by the observation that KB completion approaches fail when the majority of facts are missing for a particular relation, e.g., facts for the place of birth relation are missing for 71% of all people included in FreeBase [West et al., 2014]. Table 5.3 provides an overview of these approaches, which learn embeddings of both text and the KB, some using a joint modeling approach.

Weston et al. [2013] learn embeddings of a KB and embeddings of relation mentions in text separately, but combine the embeddings at prediction time when relations are predicted. Riedel et al. [2013] develop a joint learning approach to embed text and Freebase into the same low dimensional space. The approach is based on extensions to probabilistic models of matrix factorization and collaborative filtering. They represent their probabilistic knowledge base as a matrix with entity-entity pairs in the rows and relations in the columns. Rows come from running cross-document entity resolution across pre-existing structured databases and textual corpora. Columns come from the union of surface forms and DB relations.

Toutanova et al. [2015] learn a joint embedding model for KB entities and relations and relation mentions in text, which maps them to the same vector space. They use a convolutional neural network to derive continuous vector representations for relation mentions in text. Textual patterns are generated from dependency parsed text using a (string) sequence of words and dependency relations. The patterns are fed into a convolutional neural network which is trained jointly with the model for entities and relations from the KB. They evaluate their model on Freebase annotated with textual relation mentions. Zhong et al. [2015] jointly embed text and KB entities and relations using an alignment model which combines embeddings based on text descriptions of entities with entity embeddings based on the KB structure. For any particular entity, this alignment model makes sure that both kinds of embeddings are close in the vector space. This VSM, which is evaluated using Freebase as KB and Wikipedia as text corpus, can be used for any KB providing text descriptions for entities, e.g., Wikipedia.

Lin et al. [2015] develop a model which represents relation paths via semantic composition of relation embeddings and additionally employs a mechanism for measuring the reliability of relation paths. In the evaluation, they demonstrate the benefits of applying their KB embeddings in combination with text in a distant supervision setting, considering the task of relation extraction.

Table 5.2: Vector space models of fact KBs. Approaches are grouped by KB and task considered, and whether the approach also takes relation paths into account.

Work	KB	Paths	Task
Bordes et al. [2011]	Freebase, WordNet	no	Link prediction
Bordes et al. [2013]	Freebase, WordNet	no	Link prediction
Socher et al. [2013]	Freebase, WordNet	no	Link prediction
Yang et al. [2015]	Freebase, WordNet	no	Link prediction
Guo et al. [2015]	NELL	no	Link prediction
Ji et al. [2015]	Freebase, WordNet	no	Link prediction, triple classification
Guu et al. [2015]	Freebase, WordNet	yes	Link prediction
Neelakantan et al. [2015]	Freebase, WordNet	yes	Link prediction
Luo et al. [2015]	NELL	yes	Link prediction, triple classification

Table 5.3: Vector space models considering both fact KBs and text. Approaches are grouped by KB and task considered, and whether the approach also takes relation paths into account.

Work	KB	Paths	Task
Weston et al. [2013]	Freebase	no	Relation extraction
Riedel et al. [2013]	Freebase	no	Relation extraction
Toutanova et al. [2015]	Freebase	no	Link prediction
Lin et al. [2015]	Freebase	yes	Link prediction, Relation extraction

Lexical KBs   Only recently, embedding models have been developed that explicitly make use of lexical information present in LKBs, as opposed to fact-like information given by relation triples involving mostly named entities. Table 5.4 lists these works.

A central information type in LKBs are word senses, and most approaches to learning word embeddings do not distinguish between different word senses. Cheng et al. [2014] compare sense-disambiguated word vectors to the ambiguous word embeddings on the task of constructing vector representations of longer phrases or sentences from their component words in a compositional way. Their experiments distributional-disambiguated word vectors can possibly improve compositional methods for distributed semantics. It has to be noted though that they applied word sense induction to compute the sense disambiguated embeddings.

A straightforward approach to learning embeddings of word senses introduced by Iacobacci et al. [2015] relies on large amounts of automatically sense-annotated text and makes use of an existing program for creating word embeddings from text. Iacobacci et al. [2015] employ Babelfy to perform WSD and entity linking, i.e., word tokens in a large corpus are concatenated with their BabelNet sense identifier, and feed the modified text into the word2vec tool[1] [Mikolov et al., 2013] and thus obtain sense embeddings. Evaluated on several word similarity datasets, as well as on a relational similarity dataset [Jurgens et al., 2012], the sense embeddings outperform word embeddings, especially when the similarity computation takes an additional weighting factor into account which considers the vicinity of the two senses in the BabelNet graph.

Rothe and Schütze [2015], on the other hand, developed an embedding model for WordNet synsets and senses that explicitly accounts for the structure inherent in LKBs. Specifically, they build their model upon the assumption that words are the sum of their senses, and synsets (sets of synonymous senses) are the sum of their participating senses. These assumptions are formalized as constraints and used for learning the embeddings from the LKB WordNet.

Faruqui et al. [2015] developed a graph-based learning technique for retrofitting pretrained word embeddings to relation graphs derived from the LKBs WordNet, FrameNet, and from the *Paraphrase Database* (PPDB).[2] While their method does not aim to learn word sense embeddings, it produces semantically enriched word embeddings using relational information from several resources. The intuition behind retrofitting is to move embeddings of word types related in any of the resources closer together. As a baseline for comparison, they used a different kind of enriched word embeddings where information from LKBs is incorporated during training (e.g., [Yu and Dredze, 2014]). Evaluated on several tasks, including word and relational similarity, their retrofitted word embeddings yielded the strongest and most consistent improvements for the PPDB, followed by WordNet. FrameNet does not perform as well and even leads to worse performance; this is attributed to the fact, that FrameNet frames contain semantically more distant senses than WordNet synsets or pairs of words marked as paraphrases in the PPDB.

---

[1]http://code.google.com/p/word2vec/
[2]The PPDB [Ganitkevitch et al., 2013] is a semantic resource containing more than 220 million paraphrase pairs of English.

The embedding model by Wang et al. [2015] considers dependency parsed text distinguishing between different dependency relations, as well as relational information extracted from sense definitions (i.e., glosses) in a machine readable dictionary (they use the Online Plain Text English Dictionary). Specifically, they use the defining relation and its inverse, which is derived from sense definitions containing the headword and a defining word (e.g., one sense of the headword apple might have the sense definition *an apple is a fruit*). Both kinds of embeddings are evaluated on four word similarity datasets, showing consistent improvement compared to previous embeddings of dependency parsed text, and to embeddings learned with word2vec on raw text. Considering the fact that the embeddings of lexicographic relations have been created using only one dictionary, even better results might be possible when using LLKBs which allow aggregation of glosses from several resources for every sense.

Hermann et al. [2014] develop an embedding model for FrameNet frames using a dependency parsed corpus annotated with FrameNet frames. For each frame verbalization, their model builds a structured vector that has slots (i.e., blocks) for all dependents (i.e., dependency types) given in the dependency relation tagset. The vector for a particular predicate instance and its context is then constructed by taking the dependent heads of the predicate instance and inserting their word embeddings into these slots. Trained on a frame-annotated corpus, their model outperforms previous works on the task of FrameNet frame identification (a verb sense disambiguation task), as well as on the task of FrameNet-style SRL when combined with a standard argument identification approach.

Table 5.4: Vector space models of LKBs grouped by KB and task considered, and whether the approach also takes text into account

Work	KB	Text	Task
Hermann et al. [2014]	FrameNet	yes	FrameNet SRL
Wang et al. [2015]	MRD	yes	Word Similarity
Rothe and Schütze [2015]	WordNet	no	WSD
Faruqui et al. [2015]	WordNet, FrameNet, PPDB	no	Several tasks, including word and relational similarity
Iacobacci et al. [2015]		yes	word and relational similarity

Reflection   So far, the benefit of using linked senses in VSMs of KBs has been shown for the tasks of word similarity and relational similarity, using an approach that relies on large amounts of sense-annotated texts [Iacobacci et al., 2015]. It would be interesting to see, if the use of LLKBs in any of the other approaches discussed in Section 5.3.2 can lead to performance gains.

Compared to approaches considering fact KBs, there are fewer VSMs of LKBs, which might be due to the fact that the former play an important role in real-world applications, such as question answering. The benefit of using LKBs in NLP systems, on the other hand, is often not clearly visible and requires specialized knowledge about LKBs, which we hope to convey in this book.

5.4   CHAPTER CONCLUSION

This chapter introduced and discussed two advanced disambiguation methods: distant supervision, a paradigm in semi-supervised learning, and continuous vector space models of KBs, a technique in representation learning. Since especially the latter method is part of the rapidly evolving research in the field of Artificial Intelligence (see, e.g., the discussion about the "Deep Learning Tsunami" by Manning [2015]), our discussion of work in this area is certainly incomplete and should be understood as a partial snapshot of the state-of-the-art in October 2015.

Although there is almost no prior work yet on learning KB embeddings from LLKBs (as of October 2015), we believe that *large-scale* LLKBs, such as UBY or BabelNet, are a particularly promising type of KB for learning embeddings, mainly due to their greatly enhanced coverage. Therefore, we tried to capture previous works that are most relevant for future research on VSMs of LLKBs.

As the majority of the currently developed deep neural network architectures rely on labeled training data, we believe that the combination of distant supervision using rich knowledge sources such as LLKBs on the one hand, and VSMs of LLKB employed as features, on the other hand, is a particularly promising line of future research.

CHAPTER 6

Multilingual Applications

Another use case for LKBs are multilingual applications. This chapter covers two examples: multilingual semantic relatedness and computer-aided translation.

6.1 MULTILINGUAL SEMANTIC RELATEDNESS

Calculating the semantic similarity or relatedness of words or larger text units, such as sentences, is a core task for many NLP applications. For instance, it is a component in approaches for text reuse detection [Bär et al., 2012], textual inference [Zaenen et al., 2005], or paraphrasing [Androutsopoulos and Malakasiotis, 2010]. There are numerous datasets—both monolingual and cross-lingual ones—to test the performance of semantic similarity or relatedness calculation. While most of these datasets focus on words without any context, what is actually captured by the similarity scores is the similarity or relatedness of particular senses evoked by these words [Erbs et al., 2014].

In the rest of this section, we will use "semantic relatedness" as the broader term also covering "semantic similarity".[1] Semantically related words can thus be synonyms, hyponyms, topically related words (e.g., *Turing, computability*), or based on any other (usually semantic) relation (e.g., *singing, dancing* or *movie, star*).

Due to their concise and structured description of concepts (with sense definitions, sense relations, and sense examples), LKBs offer a natural way of deriving the semantic relatedness of word senses, and in the past, single LKBs such as WordNet [Patwardhan and Pedersen, 2006, Pilehvar et al., 2013], Wiktionary [Zesch and Gurevych, 2010, Zesch et al., 2008a], and Wikipedia [Medelyan et al., 2009, Milne and Witten, 2008] have been used for this task with great success.

There are several works that demonstrate the beneficial impact of LLKBs on the performance of relatedness calculation in the more general case of cross-lingual relatedness where the semantic relatedness of a pair of words in two languages is determined. This multilingual extension of semantic relatedness could not successfully be tackled before, because single LKBs lacked sufficient coverage.

An early approach by Agirre et al. [2009a] used the MCR to compute the cross-lingual similarity of words and obtained initial promising results.

---

[1]The difference between semantic similarity and relatedness can be explained using WordNet [Agirre et al., 2009a]: semantic similarity refers to senses (as members of synsets) that are close in the WordNet graph, whereas semantic relatedness corresponds to the observation that there exists a relation (this might be any relation) between two senses.

Meyer and Gurevych [2011] evaluated a multilingual Wiktionary-based LLKB called On-toWiktionary [Meyer and Gurevych, 2012a][2] on the tasks of monolingual and cross-lingual verb similarity. OntoWiktionary combines Wiktionary versions in English and German which were linked at the word sense level via disambiguated semantic relations and translations, i.e., OntoWiktionary provides translations between English and German at the sense level, rather than at the word level as in Wiktionary. Their results show that cross-lingual features based on the LLKB OntoWiktionary outperform the single LKBs Wiktionary and Wikipedia, and also a small LLKB consisting of WordNet and GermaNet linked at the sense level.

Navigli and Ponzetto [2012c] finally demonstrated that the rich multilingual information available in BabelNet leads to competitive results for a range of monolingual and cross-lingual word similarity datasets in several languages. Their approach uses BabelNet to construct a multilingual semantic graph by translating the two input words into all the languages available in BabelNet. They experimentally evaluated the effect of varying the number of languages used to build the multilingual networks and showed that the performance of the semantic relatedness computation increases with the number of languages used.

We conclude that LLKBs rich in multilingual information can bring about a significant boost in the performance of cross-lingual semantic relatedness calculation.

6.2   COMPUTER-AIDED TRANSLATION

In recent years, having documents available in multiple languages has turned out to be an increasingly important requirement for both institutions and individuals, e.g., governments, companies, or researchers. This raises a high demand for translation tools and resources. Statistical machine translation (SMT) systems are the predominant way to tackle this issue, but they are usually not easy to adapt to specific needs as parallel texts for training are not available for many domains. Thus, SMT systems are mainly useful during the drafting phase of the translation process, or as a quick tool for finding translations of a word or phrase. A level of translation quality which is required for official documents, such as contracts, still requires human editing [Carl et al., 2010, Koehn, 2009]. SMT systems are not sufficient for this purpose, since it is usually not easy to see what the translations actually mean and why one alternative is preferable when a probability score is all that is provided.

To produce translations of higher quality, additional tools and resources are necessary. Translation Memory systems became very popular for this purpose in the 1990s [Somers, 2003]. They provide a database of manually validated translations which can be applied if the same or a similar translation is required. They can, to some extent, deal with unseen texts via fuzzy matching, but while this approach yields a high precision, it struggles with entirely new content and is thus not useful in environments where the context changes frequently. More recently, parallel corpora have been used to identify suitable translations in context; for example, through the

---

[2]OntoWiktionary is part of UBY.

Linguee[3] service. While this might help to identify the correct translation, pinpointing the exact meaning can be hard because no sense definitions or any other lexicographic information is available. Moreover, the lack of sufficiently large parallel corpora, especially for uncommon language pairs, is also problematic.

6.2.1 OVERVIEW OF WORK IN THIS AREA

Consequently, it has been argued that multilingual lexical resources such as bilingual dictionaries or multilingual wordnets are required to provide additional knowledge. Using the information contained in those multilingual resources makes it possible to manually or (semi-)automatically determine if a translation is appropriate in context and to perform corrections. This is especially true for less common language pairs [Declerck et al., 2012, Mörth et al., 2011]. Collaboratively constructed resources such as Wiktionary or OmegaWiki allow to easily distinguish between different word senses and provide a vast amount of current lexicographic information to help identify a good translation, especially for smaller languages [Meyer, 2013], as the large body of collaborators can quickly adapt to new language phenomena like neologismsm while at the same time ensuring a remarkable quality—this phenomenon known as the "wisdom of crowds" [Surowiecki, 2005] has already been mentioned before. Expert-built resources, on the other hand, often provide additional, rather special information types. For example, WordNet focuses on synsets and their taxonomy, but mostly disregards syntactic information, which is in turn the focus of VerbNet. However, their enormous building effort is the reason why for many smaller languages such resources remain small or do not even exist. This is why a combination of both collaborative and expert-built resources is a promising endeavor to combine both their strengths.

Human translators traditionally utilize monolingual and bilingual dictionaries as a reference. Dictionaries provide many different kinds of lexicographic information, such as sense definitions, example sentences, collocations, idioms, etc. They are well crafted for being used by humans, but using them computationally poses a great challenge. Although machine readable dictionaries can be processed automatically, computers are often challenged to properly interpret the structure of an entry or resolve ambiguities that are intuitively clear to humans.

The great success of the Princeton WordNet motivated the creation of a large number of multilingual wordnets, such as the already discussed *EuroWordNet* [Vossen, 1998], *BalkaNet* [Stamou et al., 2002], *MultiWordNet* [Pianta et al., 2002], or *Open Multilingual Wordnet* [Bond and Foster, 2013]. While the nature of these resources seems to perfectly meet the requirements of computer-aided translation, only few of them gained a size comparable to the English WordNet or provide as many different information types as dictionaries (such as etymology, pronunciation or derived terms) due to their time-consuming and costly construction process.

Creating such a resource requires expertise in linguistics, which makes the process expensive and time-consuming, which, in turn, poses significant limitations on resource growth and update rates. Automatically induced resources based on the output of Open Information Extrac-

---

[3]http://www.linguee.com

tion (OIE) systems such as *KnowItAll* [Banko et al., 2007] can be huge and kept up to date at any time. However, those resources are not sense disambiguated *per se* and, due to the completely automatic creation process, limited in their quality.

There exists a significant amount of work using Wikipedia in the context of cross-lingual information retrieval for query expansion or query translation [Gaillard et al., 2010, Herbert et al., 2011, Potthast et al., 2008], and also as a parallel corpus [Adafre and de Rijke, 2006] or as a source for mining bilingual terminology [Erdmann et al., 2009]. However, it is primarily an encyclopedic resource, which limits the amount of lexical knowledge available for parts of speech other than nouns. Translators also require lexicographic information types such as idioms, collocations, or usage examples as well as translations for word classes other than nouns—most importantly verbs, adjectives, and adverbs. Müller and Gurevych [2009] discuss combining Wiktionary and Wikipedia for cross-lingual information retrieval, but in this case Wiktionary is also merely used for query expansion and most of the lexicographic knowledge encoded in it remains disregarded. This knowledge is essential for translation applications in order to make well-grounded decisions.

Consequently, the usage of large-scale LLKBs was also considered in this area, as they combine the strengths of the singular LKBs (see Table 6.1). BabelNet [Navigli and Ponzetto, 2012a], for instance, contains not only multilingual information from Wikipedia, but also from Wiktionary and OmegaWiki. While BabelNet also does not include all information from the stand-alone resources which might be useful for this application scenario, it additionally provides automatically added translations for a large amount of languages, which (different from classical SMT systems) are attached to particular word senses. While BabelNet has not been directly applied to translation applications, it was successfully used for cross-lingual WSD [Navigli and Ponzetto, 2012b]. Matuschek et al. [2013] describe the usage of UBY (which also contains the multilingual LKBs OmegaWiki, Wiktionary, and Wikipedia) for translation applications, however, they do not present a functional system, which would be the next necessary step to truly leverage the multilingual knowledge contained therein.

Reflection   In general, the usage of LLKBs for translation applications has the following immediate advantages.

- Better coverage as the lexemes and senses from all resources can be considered. This is generally true for all applications which utilize LLKBs.

- Complementary information such as additional example sentences or context information for a sense which helps choosing the correct translation.

- Better structured translation results achieved, for instance, by clustering the translations into the same language for linked senses instead of simply considering all of them in parallel.

- Identical translations in different resources yield combined evidence and thus higher translation confidence.

Table 6.1: Comparison of the advantages of different resource types (OIE = Open Information Extraction)

Resource Type	Information Types	Lexicon Size	Usage for NLP	Update Time	Quality
Dictionaries	many	considerable	hard	long	very high
Wordnets	limited	small	easy	long	very high
OIE-based	many	huge	easy	short	low
Wikipedia	encyclopedic	large	medium	short	high
Wiktionary	many	large	medium	short	high
OmegaWiki	many	medium	easy	short	high
BabelNet, UBY	many	huge	easy	short	high

6.2.2 ILLUSTRATIVE EXAMPLE

To illustrate the advantages of using linked senses, we will consider one example described by Matuschek et al. [2013] which is taken from the greater context of UBY: the alignment between Wiktionary and OmegaWiki. Particularly interesting in this case is that, as OmegaWiki is a multilingual resource by design, there exists a linking to multilingual synsets. This means that the (disambiguated) translations encoded apply to the aligned Wiktionary senses. This entails that the correct translation is immediately known once the word sense in the source document can be correctly identified (either by the user or by automatic word sense disambiguation). A similar argument also holds for Wiktionary—all linked senses from OmegaWiki benefit from the additional translations available in Wiktionary. The only disadvantage in this case is that these are not disambiguated. An illustration of this scenario is given in Figure 6.1.

As an example for the noun *bass*, the word sense "A male singer who sings in the deepest vocal range" from OmegaWiki is linked to the sense "A male singer who sings in the bass range" from Wiktionary. While these two different definitions might themselves be useful for pinpointing the exact meaning of the term depending on the context, there are a number of further valuable information sources.

- Wiktionary offers translations into Spanish, Dutch, Bulgarian, Tatar, Finnish, German, Greek, Hungarian, Italian, Japanese, Russian, and Slovene, while OmegaWiki additionally encodes translations into French, Georgian, Korean and Portuguese. Only the Spanish translation *bajo* and the Italian translation *basso* are included in both. Thus, the link directly yields a significantly broader range of translations than either resource alone.

- OmegaWiki offers sense definitions of this word sense in Spanish and French which are useful for a translator fluent in one of these languages. Moreover, the Spanish sense

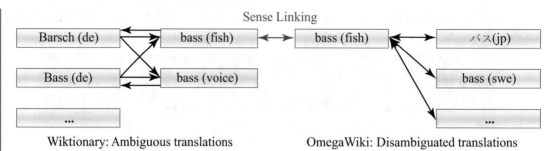

Figure 6.1: Illustration of the sense linking between Wiktionary and OmegaWiki. As the translations in OmegaWiki are unambiguous, they directly apply to the aligned Wiktionary sense. Although this is not the case for the translations in Wiktionary, they still offer additional translation options. The ambiguity in Wiktionary is exemplified by the arrows pointing from German *Barsch* and *Bass* to both English senses of *bass*—there is no explicit link to the correct sense, only to the lexeme.

definition from OmegaWiki can directly be used to identify the correct sense of the Spanish translation, which is not disambiguated in Wiktionary.

- Wiktionary also offers additional information not included in OmegaWiki, such as etymology, pronunciation, and derived terms.

Table 6.2 summarizes the information that becomes available through the linking between Wiktionary and OmegaWiki for *bass*.

Table 6.2: Information gain through the linking for one sense of *bass*

Resource	Translation Languages	Available Definitions	Additional Information Types
Wiktionary	12	1	5
OmegaWiki	6	3	0
Combined	16	4	5

While this is only an illustrative example, Matuschek et al. [2013] provide further statistics about both single resources as well as their combination. Even with only 2 languages and 2 resources considered, they obtain 1,600,000 translations. For the whole resource UBY, the number is an order of magnitude higher, due to the integration of Wikipedia and further cross-lingual links between monolingual resources.

6.3   CHAPTER CONCLUSION

In this chapter, we presented two examples of multilingual applications that benefit from LLKBs: multilingual semantic relatedness as a fundamental task in NLP applications, and computer-aided translation.

We have seen that the use of BabelNet as a LLKB especially rich in multilingual information leads to a performance boost in multilingual semantic relatedness by making use of information from all languages in BabelNet jointly. Computer-aided translation, a use case directly involving humans, was illustrated with the LLKB UBY. We conjecture that UBY is better suited for this use case than BabelNet, because human translators usually appreciate transparency, e.g., regarding the provenance of the translations. UBY is designed in a way that preserves the integrated LKBs and the source of the translations, and thus offers more transparency as BabelNet.

There are many more multilingual applications in the context of LLKBs waiting to be explored. For example, the application of multilingual relatedness in end-to-end tasks, such as multilingual multi-document summarization might be an interesting direction for future research.

CHAPTER 7

Interfaces and Tools

7.1 EXPLORATION INTERFACES

While easy programmatic access to linked LKBs is crucial for employing them in NLP tasks (as we will explain in Section 7.3), the initial step of determining their added value for particular tasks is a challenge in itself, because it is not intuitively clear what kind of information is available in what resource and how it can be related and exploited by human users and machines. In other words, what is required are tools for qualitative and exploratory examination of the linked resources.

Web interfaces have been long used for accessing electronic dictionaries, such as the *Oxford Dictionary of English* or the *American Heritage Dictionary* [Lew, 2011]. These interfaces have also largely influenced the development of web interfaces for LKBs, such as the ones for WordNet, FrameNet, Wiktionary, or *DANTE* [Kilgarriff, 2010] which directly built upon the dictionary interface models. Two other examples for accessing WordNet are *Visuwords*[1] and *WordNet explorer*[2] that allow browsing of the WordNet synset structure. Kunze and Lemnitzer [2002] present a similar interface for browsing GermaNet. An example for a cross-lingual graph-based interface is *VisualThesaurus*[3] which shows related words in six different languages. The *Korp* interface allows easy access of the Swedish Språkbanken [Borin et al., 2012], while the *VisDic* interface of the BalkaNet project [Horak and Smrz, 2004] allows to not only browse the contained information, but also to edit it, which makes it a rare exception in the area of expert-built resources.

Most of these interfaces, however, have been designed in adherence to a specific, single LKB, and only a few are able to display information from multiple heterogeneous sources. The majority of them are limited to show preformatted lexical entries one after another without making any attempt to connect them. Popular examples are *Dictionary.com*[4] and *TheFreeDictionary*.[5] Similarly, the *DWDS* interface [Klein and Geyken, 2010] displays its entries in small rearrangeable boxes. The *Wörterbuchnetz* [Burch and Rapp, 2007] is an example of a web interface that connects its entries by hyperlinks—however, only at the level of lemmas and not word senses.

Interfaces to collaboratively constructed resources have been discussed in detail in Section 1.2, as for them the construction paradigm and the interfaces are intimately connected—the Wiki interfaces directly shape the way the knowledge is structured, so that interface and representation format essentially become one. While there have been different attempts to make user

---

[1]http://www.visuwords.com
[2]http://faculty.uoit.ca/collins/research/wnVis.html
[3]http://www.visualthesaurus.com
[4]http://www.dictionary.com
[5]http://www.thefreedictionary.com

interfaces more convenient and accessible, the Wiki markup has still prevailed as the most widely accepted means of displaying the content due to its flexibility.

In general, however, most work in the past focused either on the allowing access to single resources (or a single type of resource), or on the integration of several resources in proprietary and heterogeneous formats. On top of that, complete UI access was rarely provided for integrated resources, which follows immediately from the heterogeneous ways in which access to the single LKBs has been realized. As a result, the comparative exploration of different LKBs, and in particular, of sense-aligned LKBs in order to assess their quality and usefulness for particular tasks is not easy in practice; neither is their orchestrated usage. This makes it hard for the community to exploit them on a large scale, diminishing the impact that these projects might achieve.

To alleviate this, the two outstanding LLKB projects we have discussed earlier, Babel-Net and UBY, have also put significant work into this aspect of the resources, in order to make the extensive amount of knowledge contained therein accessible to a wider audience. The *Babel-NetXplorer* [Navigli and Ponzetto, 2012e] enables access to the semantic network in BabelNet in different ways. The starting point is usually a single lemma, for which a list of different senses is returned, including a definition and pictures if available (Figure 7.1). As BabelNet bakes information from different sources into *Babel Synsets*, it is not immediately visible which piece of information comes from which source at this point.

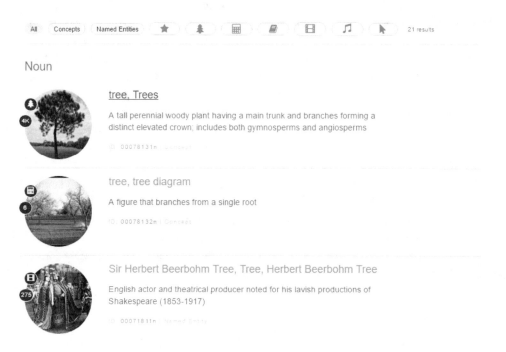

Figure 7.1: A list of concepts in the BabelNetXplorer.

A much more detailed view becomes available once a single sense is selected (Figure 7.2). Now, information such as translations, pronunciation, and categories are visible, and in this view it is also possible to reveal the sources of the single information items. This perspective is also directly linked to the *Babelfy* interface [Moro et al., 2014b], which allows to directly perform WSD with BabelNet as a sense inventory.

Figure 7.2: A single concept in the BabelNetXplorer.

The core element of BabelNetXplorer is the flexible graphical view, which offers a stream-lined way to easily navigate the full BabelNet graph, and also allows jumping back to the text-centered view of a single concept in order to explore further (Figure 7.3). The semantic graph of BabelNet is also the foundation of *BabelRelate* [Navigli and Ponzetto, 2012c], a toolkit for calculating semantic relatedness which is also anchored in the same ecosystem.

An initial version of the web interface to UBY [Gurevych et al., 2012b] offers a graph-based visualization of sense linkings between the integrated LKBs. Different senses of the same lemma which are linked across LKBs are grouped via *alignment nodes* so that the source of the infor-

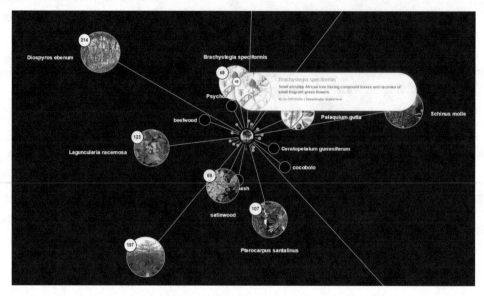

Figure 7.3: The graph view of the BabelNetXplorer.

mation as well as the richness of the sense representation becomes apparent via descriptions and color-coding. This allows exploring and assessing the individual senses across resource boundaries. Accompanying this, there is also a textual view for examining lexical information in detail. For a given lemma, all senses available in UBY can be retrieved and the information attached to them can be inspected. In this detailed view, it is also possible to navigate to other senses by following the hyperlinks, e.g., for following sense alignments across resources or semantic relations within a LKB. Additionally, the user can compare any two senses in a detailed side-by-side view. For linked senses, this enables the immediate discovery and examination of complementary lexical information from different LKBs. As the information is presented in a uniform way (due to the standard-compliant representation of UBY), a user can easily compare the information available from different LKBs without having to use different tools, terminologies, and UIs.

The visualization of sense linkings in the initial version of the UBY web interface was subject to a subsequent analysis and redesign in collaboration with a visualization expert [Eckle-Kohler et al., 2014]. This redesign was the result of a detailed requirements analysis with respect to the targeted user groups in the two fields of NLP and Digital Humanities. A particular issue of the initial graph-based visualization was a lack of scalability for lemmas with a large number of senses and sense links. The final, revised version of the visualization component uses cluster-based design, which groups linked senses within a cluster enclosed in a circle, and orders the senses inside each cluster according to resources. Figure 7.4 shows the final cluster-based design.

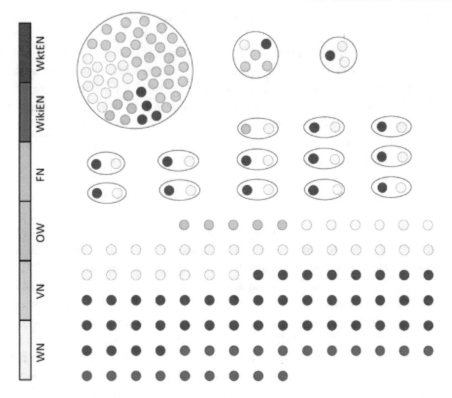

Figure 7.4: Cluster-based visualization of sense links for the lemma *run* from the LLKB UBY.

Note that for all interfaces considering linked or merged resources, interoperability issues have to be addressed in a comprehensive way—these issues have been discussed in more detail in Section 1.3.

7.2 CURATION INTERFACES

Apart from the mere access to LKBs, another point which has recently received additional interest is their curation—that is, the editing process after the initial creation which aims at correcting errors and adding new content. For the longest time, this was no issue, as curation of LKBs was largely a task for a closed group of experts (see Section 1.1), so that the editing process usually relied on makeshift tools and interfaces, and most often the underlying files were edited manually. However, with the advent of collaboratively constructed resources, the topic of making knowledge not only accessible, but also editable, came more into focus. Resources like Wikipedia, Wiktionary, and OmegaWiki were explicitly designed with the possibility in mind that everyone can edit them, and the underlying Wiki technology is deeply intertwined with their philosophy, most obviously expressed by their names. These interfaces have been presented in greater detail in Section 1.2.

In the related field of linguistic corpus annotation, it has been recognized early on that experts should be able to edit or create content based on user interfaces, as the work load would be too hard to handle otherwise. While crowdsourcing has also been used in this field [Fossati et al., 2013], linguistic corpus annotation tasks are still primarily carried out by experts, resulting in corpora of highly limited size. That is to say, there is currently a wide variety of web-based annotation tools available for the creation of copora by experts, such as BRAT [Stenetorp et al., 2012], the Groningen Meaning Bank Explorer [Basile et al., 2012a], WebAnno [Yimam et al., 2013], and CSniper [Eckart de Castilho et al., 2012], and these tools make the annotation easier (or possible), but another aspect which has been largely disregarded until recently is the motivation for contributing to such a project.

Regarding LKBs, it is mostly clear why experts invest the time and resources for LKB creation, but the motivation for projects such as Wiktionary is a topic of research in itself—which is outside the scope of this book. Nevertheless, especially for large-scale LKBs, it is now widely accepted that it is necessary to draw a larger crowd of people which are not per se linguistically inclined. To this end, one suggestion is to "gamify" the curation, i.e., make the otherwise tedious editing process less exhausting by wrapping it into some kind of entertaining, competitive or otherwise motivating environment. This kind of gamification has already been suggested for the related areas of crowd-based corpus annotation [Chklovski and Mihalcea, 2002, Seemakurty et al., 2010, Venhuizen et al., 2013], anaphora resolution [Hladká et al., 2009, Poesio et al., 2013], paraphrasing [Chklovski and Gil, 2005], term associations [Artignan et al., 2009, Lafourcade and Joubert, 2010], and query expansion [Simko et al., 2011].

Especially with the involvement of automatic number in the construction of large-scale LLKBs, which inevitably introduce a certain amount of errors, it is now more necessary than ever to think about effective corresponding motivational techniques. Attempts using "regular" crowdsourcing [Biemann and Nygaard, 2010, Eom et al., 2012, Sarasua et al., 2012] had only very limited success, so that gamification gains more and more attention. In the context of adding descriptive labels to images on the web, von Ahn and Dabbish [2004] generate common sense facts by using a game similar to Taboo. Rzeniewicz and Szymański [2013] extends WordNet with common-sense knowledge using a questions-based game, and Siorpaes and Hepp [2008] present a game which aims to classify Wikipedia pages as either categories or individual entities. Disadvantages of these suggestions are that they are all based on text interfaces, hence lacking the attraction of "real" games, and that most often at least two players are required. Vannella et al. [2014] present pioneering work to alleviate these shortcomings. They propose two single-player video games (a top-down shooter and a role-playing game) for validating associations between concepts, and between concepts and images. They show that these games are intrinsically motivating, i.e., no external incentive is required, and that the curation quality is competitive with non-gaming approaches. Nevertheless, it is clear that such games are very costly in their production, so that flexibility with regard to different LKBs and tasks is necessary to make the effort worthwhile.

7.3   RESOURCE API'S FOR TEXT PROCESSING

A further important factor to the success of a LKB in NLP research is a public API (Application Programming Interface), which facilitates programmatic access. A good example how this can work is the API for the most popular single resource, WordNet. The Java WordNet Library[6] is widely used and well developed, as is the Java-based Wikipedia API,[7] which not only allows programmatic access to current Wikipedia content, but also to the link structure, discussion pages and revisions, i.e., past states of articles—this has been widely exploited for different research tasks [Daxenberger and Gurevych, 2013, Daxenberger et al., 2012]. In the same line of work, similar APIs for Wiktionary[8] and OmegaWiki[9] have been developed. Also for GermaNet, a constantly updated Java-API[10] exists. All of these APIs are freely available, and they all have been developed with only one LKB in mind, i.e., they have been carefully created to make the knowledge available as complete and convenient as possible, with the trade-off of accommodating idiosyncrasies in formalisms and data formats.

However, the rise of large-scale LLKBs—which has extensively been discussed in this book—calls for a broader perspective on the programmatic access to these resources. With the overwhelming amount of information, and also information types, easy access to sense-linked LKBs is crucial for their acceptance and use in NLP, as only then their full potential can be leveraged. While single LKBs and their APIs are reasonably well understood, researchers face the problem of using them in an orchestrated manner. With this in mind, corresponding APIs have been created for the two most popular LLKBs which we have previously presented: UBY and BabelNet.

For convenient access to UBY, a Java-based API built around the Hibernate framework was developed, which allows a quick change between representation formats as required by the particular application: Java objects, XML, or SQL database entires. The main design principle is to directly represent instances of the underlying UBY-LMF data model, providing methods for direct access to their attributes and related objects. On top of this, there exists a large amount of convenience methods to aggregate information which is related, but spread out over several classes: this is internally realized via joint database tables which are temporarily stored in memory after the first access. For instance, it is possible to directly iterate over all lexical entries (and their senses) with a particular part of speech.

Another important design aspect has been to ensure that the functionality of the individual, resource-specific APIs (or user interfaces) can be mirrored with the UBY-API. This is meant to

---

[6]http://sourceforge.net/projects/jwordnet/
[7]http://code.google.com/p/jwpl/
[8]https://code.google.com/p/jwktl/
[9]https://code.google.com/p/jowkl/
[10]http://www.sfs.uni-tuebingen.de/lsd/tools.shtml

enable the use of legacy applications with the LLKB UBY. As an example, see the corresponding UBY-API operations for the most important operations in the WordNet API in Table 7.1. A notable aspect here is that the naming conventions change, while the content remains the same. For instance, an `IndexWord` in WordNet becomes a `LexicalEntry` in UBY. This harmonization of the terminology is due to the uniform terminology defined in the UBY-LMF data model. The true benefit of using such a LLKB, however, only becomes visible when multiple resources are queried to get a single combined result—demonstrating the increase in lexical and sense coverage, as well as the enrichment of sense representations based on the sense links.

Table 7.1:   Some equivalent operations in the WordNet-API and the UBY-API

WordNet Function	UBY Function
Dictionary	**UBY**
getIndexWord(pos, lemma)	getLexicalEntries(pos, lemma)
IndexWord	**LexicalEntry**
getLemma()	getLemmaForm()
Synset	**Synset**
getGloss()	getDefinitionText()
getWords()	getSenses()
Pointer	**SynsetRelation**
getType()	getRelName()
Word	**Sense**
getPointers()	getSenseRelations()

For the other large-scale LLKB, BabelNet, the *BabelNet API* [Navigli and Ponzetto, 2012d] has been developed, which is specifically tailored toward multilingual usage scenarios. The API is based on Apache Lucene, which is used for indexing the textual representation of BabelNet, and it includes several methods to access lexicographic and encyclopedic information about concepts, the relations between them, as well as translations. A major design goal was to accomplish complex knowledge extraction tasks with as little code as possible.

Besides that, the BabelNet API is also designed as a framework for multilingual graph-based lexical disambiguation, i.e., WSD based on the semantic connections found in the LKB. To this end, the API allows to create and store semantic graphs, and to perform a depth-first search in these graphs up to a predefined maximum depth. These paths are stored within a Lucene index for efficient lookup of those paths starting and ending in a specific synset. Given a set of ambiguous words as input, the API then looks for their connecting paths and merges such paths within a single graph to disambiguate them. This process can also be further parametrized to account for aspects like different edge weights, and the graph nodes can also be scored using a variety of methods, such as their PageRank value, in turn better leveraging the structure of the underlying

LKB. This is especially interesting, as the WSD engine generally allows to use resources other than BabelNet—for instance, this has been tested for WordNet, and as long as the graph structure of a LKB can be mapped to the corresponding Java classes, a relatively straightforward integration should be possible.

Finally, a recent trend is to move away from locally stored resources and databases and corresponding APIs and instead make the information available in online repositories and through web services, like in the Linguistic Linked Open Data Cloud which has already been discussed in Section 1.3. The idea is to abstract away from idiosyncratic data structures and instead to offer the data via established standards such as HTML and JSON. The foundation for these services are generic semantic representation models such as *lemon* [McCrae et al., 2011]. In this way, access to the data is possible in any programming language or framework. Many of the resources discussed in this book (for instance, WordNet, Wiktionary, and Wikipedia) are already available through the LLOD, and also for integrated resources like UBY efforts have been made to make them accessible [Eckle-Kohler et al., 2015].

7.4   CHAPTER CONCLUSION

In this chapter, we discussed three distinct aspects of accessing the knowledge contained in LLKBs.

First of all, we presented an overview of exploration interfaces which allow to manually assess and inspect the contents of a resource, which is often a crucial entry point for research efforts. In particular, we have described the evolution from makeshift textual interfaces for singular resources to graphical interfaces for large-scale linked resources which are highly interactive and responsive and especially enable the exploration of the underlying graph structures.

After that, we also discussed different approaches to curate resources, i.e., edit and correct them. The vanguard for this direction of research were the Wiki interfaces introduced with resources like Wikipedia and Wiktionary. These aim to make curation of knowledge accessible to anyone, and this trend is also likely to affect expert-built resources, which traditionally have been walled gardens.

Finally, we briefly introduced various APIs for accessing LKBs programmatically, which for instance can be used for end user applications or more sophisticated data-driven research efforts. While many of the resources presented in this issue have been made available in this way for particular programming languages and environments, the inevitable (and exciting) direction for the future is to offer resources online, in generic representation formats and based on established standards. The goal is to make them accessible to as many people as possible with the least effort.

CHAPTER 8

Conclusion and Outlook

8.1 SUMMARY

Linked lexical knowledge bases are nowadays one of the most exciting and promising directions for knowledge-driven NLP, as they enable the combination of a multitude of different knowledge types and languages to empower all kinds of applications. In this book, we set out and discussed the building blocks of LLKBs, the motivations and paradigms for their construction, as well as methods and applications where the usage of LLKBs brings about particular benefits.

For the introduction and discussion of LKBs in Chapter 1, we started with a definition of what a lexical knowledge base is, and what different kinds of information LKBs usually contain. For the discussion of the actual LKBs, we distinguished between expert-built and collaboratively constructed ones, and put a special focus on the particular information types and structural peculiarities each of them provides. We found that there are many remarkable differences between LKBs, which is the underlying motivation for combining them in LLKBs. We also covered aspects of the standardization of LKBs. This has become an increasingly important topic in the endeavor to combine resources and make them easily available, as in the past, proprietary file formats and idiosyncratic design decisions were a major obstacle. We introduced the major standard LMF, which has found many adopters, as well as modeling techniques established in context of the Semantic Web.

To prepare the discussion of existing LLKBs, we first defined the notion of sense linking in Chapter 2. Subsequently, we presented the large-scale LLKBs which form the current state-of-the-art, such as UBY and BabelNet, but also past attempts to create linked resources, which most often involved only two or three LKBs. These are especially interesting with regard to the motivation for their construction, and in a way, they paved the ground for the larger LLKBs UBY and BabelNet. We also briefly touched on the issue of manual linking of resources, which is especially relevant for collaborative efforts.

The majority of linkings between resources, however, is created automatically, which is why we dedicated an entire chapter to linking algorithms (Chapter 3). In order to allow the reader to fully comprehend the task of WSL and see it in a greater context, we first outlined the common and distinctive traits with regard to related information integration tasks in NLP and other fields. Thereby, we established that WSL has unique requirements which have to be considered when designing algorithmic approaches for this challenge. For instance, one usually cannot rely on well-defined structures or instance-based matching as it is common for ontologies or database schemata. After that, we presented linking algorithms based on the two perennial information sources available in LKBs: textual descriptions of senses (i.e., glosses) and the LKB structure, induced by semantic relations or links. We discussed the strengths and weaknesses of different approaches for each of these two general directions, and we also described ideas which combine similarity-based and graph-based measures for WSL and thereby achieve the best results thus far across languages and resource types.

To substantiate the motivation for linking different knowledge bases, we presented methods and applications which benefit from sense linkings in three dedicated chapters. In Chapter 4, we explained how the disambiguation of textual units, a cornerstone task in NLP, benefits from the richer structure and combined knowledge in LLKBs, and from clustering fine-grained word senses by exploiting 1:n links. Next in Chapter 5, we discussed the use of LLKBs in the context of two especially promising knowledge-based approaches in machine learning. These are the more recent methods of distant supervision and neural vector space models of KBs. Both methods play an important role for automatic training data generation based on LLKBs. Thirdly, we covered examples of multilingual applications in Chapter 6, in particular computer-aided translation, where we argued that the collaboratively constructed multilingual LKBs can be valuable sources of additional translations and other kinds of knowledge for this kind of applications.

Chapter 7 finally considered the question how LLKBs can be explored and edited via interfaces, and also how they can be accessed via APIs. While there has been a large amount of work in these directions in the past, with the rise of tremendously large and complex linked resources this issue becomes more and more pertinent.

8.2   OUTLOOK

This book attempts to comprehensively cover the current state-of-the-art in the construction and use of linked lexical knowledge bases, and thus aims to provide a basis for future work in this area. There are many avenues for future work, as LLKBs are relatively new knowledge sources and many researchers in NLP have focused their efforts in the last decade elsewhere, especially in data-driven and, more recently, in neural networks approaches.

In the rest of this section, we will outline just some of the many possible directions. Most obviously, as one of dominating themes is creating *large-scale* sense-linked LKB, a perennial topic is the consideration of further resource pairs for linking, in order to achieve larger and more densely linked resources. While, arguably, not all possible links seem sensible,[1] it will continue to be vital to identify those LKB combinations which might be beneficial for language processing, and have interesting properties motivating further investigations with regard to the algorithmic approaches. This involves closer examination of resources that proved challenging to align automatically (such as VerbNet), investigation of resources disregarded thus far and also coverage of new resources which might emerge in the future, especially automatically created ones, such as the paraphrase database. For these, their content and structure have to be analyzed with regard

---

[1]For instance, there is no conceivable immediate incentive to link Wikipedia to VerbNet, as they exclusively contain different parts of speech; however, the perpetual evaluation of possible application scenarios might prove us wrong in time.

to their applicability within the existing similarity- and graph-based frameworks. This especially includes further experiments on cross-lingual alignments, a topic which only has been briefly touched thus far and holds great potential for new combinations.

Regarding extensions of the algorithmic linking approaches, one of the most obvious directions for progress is the investigation of further similarity measures. Text similarity is a very active field of research in its own right, and frameworks like DKPro-Similarity [Bär et al., 2013] which implement a plethora of complex (and also combined) measures might lead to further improvements. But also the integration of similarity measures operating on neural vector representations seems to be particularly promising in this context.

For graph-based approaches, a main issue to address is the improvement of the graph density, which is an issue especially for collaboratively constructed resources. Laparra et al. [2010] discuss a possibility to do this with high precision, where the main idea is to focus on lexemes with a low degree of polysemy and align them if one of the possible target senses is clearly more similar to the source sense than the other(s). If recall is still low, more polysemous lexemes can be examined. Pilehvar and Navigli [2014] adopt and extend this idea of polysemous linking to further improve their WSL approach we discussed earlier.

A weighting of edges (e.g., based on gloss similarities) has only rarely been considered, but would be easily applicable. The combination of graph distances and similarities has already proven effective for the combined approaches, and it would be interesting to see how an even closer interweaving of these notions might be beneficial. It might also be interesting to investigate whether integration of joint knowledge from several LKBs might be helpful. For instance, the information that two senses in resources A and B share a strong resemblance to senses in another resource C could be expressed by additional features in a machine learning approach. An even more elaborate idea would be to investigate entirely different graph-based algorithms, e.g., for matching nodes in bipartite graphs.

Apart from the work directly concerning the linkings, infrastructure-related aspects of LLKBs such as APIs and interfaces will continue to be an important topic. There will always be errors resulting from automatic linking, no matter how precise the algorithm is, so that improved editing and curation interfaces will be necessary to improve the quality of large-scale LLKBs—we have discussed gamification as one particularly interesting direction in this area. Another goal is to enhance the visualization of links across multiple resources to ease the usage, especially for laymen or for researchers yet unfamiliar with these kinds of resources, for instance, in the humanities.

Regarding the use of LLKBs in NLP, there is a lot of potential for further knowledge-based applications waiting to be explored, beyond the examples we presented here. For example, in the field of information retrieval, the usage of KBs is commonly suggested, e.g., for indexing [Deerwester et al., 1990], for domain-specific information retrieval [Müller and Gurevych, 2009], or semantic relatedness calculation [Otegi et al., 2014]. Also for other semantic tasks such as recognizing textual entailment, which strongly rely on the semantic relations between word senses,

LLKBs might lead to significant improvements, especially in combination with lexical inference knowledge automatically extracted from large corpora.

Acronyms

- **AKBC** Automatic Knowledge Base Construction
- **API** Application Programming Interface
- **IR** Information Retrieval
- **KB** Knowledge Base
- **LKB** Lexical Knowledge Base
- **LLKB** Linked Lexical Knowledge Base
- **LMF** Lexical Markup Framework
- **LU** Lexical Unit
- **MFS** Most Frequent Sense
- **MRD** Machine Readable Dictionary
- **NLP** Natural Language Processing
- **OIE** Open Information Extraction
- **POS** Part of Speech
- **PPR** Personalized PageRank
- **RDF** Resource Description Framework
- **SMT** Statistical Machine Translation
- **SRL** Semantic Role Labeling
- **VSM** Vector Space Model
- **WSD** Word Sense Disambiguation
- **WSA** Word Sense Alignment
- **WSL** Word Sense Linking

Bibliography

Sisay Fissaha Adafre and Maarten de Rijke. Finding Similar Sentences across Multiple Languages in Wikipedia. In *Proc. of the Workshop "New Text: Wikis and Blogs and Other Dynamic Text Sources"*, pages 62–69, Trento, Italy, 2006. 70

Eneko Agirre and Oier Lopez de Lacalle. Clustering WordNet Word Senses. In *Proc. of the International Conference on Recent Advances in Natural Language Processing*, pages 11–18, Borovets, Bulgaria, 2003. DOI: 10.1075/cilt.260.13agi. 51

Eneko Agirre and Aitor Soroa. SemEval-2007 Task 02: Evaluating Word Sense Induction and Discrimination Systems. In *Proc. of the 4th International Workshop on Semantic Evaluations*, pages 7–12, Prague, Czech Republic, 2007. DOI: 10.3115/1621474.1621476. 48

Eneko Agirre and Aitor Soroa. Personalizing PageRank for Word Sense Disambiguation. In *Proc. of the 12th Conference of the European Chapter of the Association for Computational Linguistics (EACL)*, pages 33–41, Athens, Greece, 2009. DOI: 10.3115/1609067.1609070. 33, 34, 35, 47

Eneko Agirre, Enrique Alfonseca, Keith Hall, Jana Kravalova, Marius Pasca, and Aitor Soroa. A Study on Similarity and Relatedness Using Distributional and WordNet-Based Approaches. In *Proc. of Human Language Technologies 2009: The Conference of the North American Chapter of the Association for Computational Linguistics (NAACL-HLT)*, pages 19–27, Boulder, CO, 2009a. DOI: 10.3115/1620754.1620758. 67

Eneko Agirre, Oier Lopez De Lacalle, and Aitor Soroa. Knowledge-Based WSD on Specific Domains: Performing Better than Generic Supervised WSD. In *Proc. of the 21th International Joint Conference on Artificial Intelligence (IJCAI)*, pages 1501–1506, Pasadena, CA, 2009b. 47

Eneko Agirre, Oier Lopez de Lacalle, and Aitor Soroa. Random Walks for Knowledge-Based Word Sense Disambiguation. *Computational Linguistics*, 40(1), pages 57–84, 2014. DOI: 10.1162/coli_a_00164. 49

Ion Androutsopoulos and Prodromos Malakasiotis. A Survey of Paraphrasing and Textual Entailment Methods. *Journal of Artificial Intelligence Research*, 38(1), pages 135–187, 2010. DOI: 10.1162/10.1613/jair.2985. 67

Guillaume Artignan, Mountaz Hascoet, and Mathieu Lafourcade. Multiscale Visual Analysis of Lexical Networks. In *Information Visualisation, 2009 13th International Conference*, pages 685–690, 2009. DOI: 10.1109/iv.2009.100. 80

Vikraman Arvind, Johannes Köbler, Sebastian Kuhnert, and Yadu Vasudev. Approximate Graph Isomorphism. In Branislav Rovan, Vladimiro Sassone, and Peter Widmayer, Eds., *Mathematical Foundations of Computer Science*, vol. 7464 of *Lecture Notes in Computer Science*, pages 100–111, Springer, Berlin/Heidelberg, 2012. DOI: 10.1007/bfb0029591. 32

Sue B. T. Atkins and Michael Rundell. *The Oxford Guide to Practical Lexicography*. Oxford University Press, Oxford, 2008. 3

Jordi Atserias, Luís Villarejo, German Rigau, Eneko Agirre, John Carroll, Bernardo Magnini, and Piek Vossen. The Meaning Multilingual Central Repository. In *Proc. of the 2nd International Global WordNet Conference*, pages 23–30, Brno, Czech Republic, 2004. 26

Mohammed Attia, Lamia Tounsi, and Josef van Genabith. Automatic Lexical Resource Acquisition for Constructing an LMF-Compatible Lexicon of Modern Standard Arabic. Technical report, Dublin, Ireland, 2010. 18

Stefano Baccianella, Andrea Esuli, and Fabrizio Sebastiani. SentiWordNet 3.0: An Enhanced Lexical Resource for Sentiment Analysis and Opinion Mining. In *Proc. of the 7th International Conference on Language Resources and Evaluation (LREC)*, pages 2200–2204, La Valetta, Malta, 2010. 5

Collin F. Baker and Christiane Fellbaum. WordNet and FrameNet as Complementary Resources for Annotation. In *Proc. of the 3rd Linguistic Annotation Workshop*, pages 125–129, Suntec, Singapore, 2009. DOI: 10.3115/1698381.1698402. 19, 26

Collin F. Baker, Charles J. Fillmore, and John B. Lowe. The Berkeley FrameNet Project. In *Proc. of the 36th Annual Meeting of the Association for Computational Linguistics and 17th International Conference on Computational Linguistics*, pages 86–90, Montreal, Canada, 1998. DOI: 10.3115/980845.980860. 6

Timothy Baldwin, Su Nam Kim, Francis Bond, Sanae Fujita, David Martinez, and Takaaki Tanaka. A Reexamination of MRD-Based Word Sense Disambiguation. *ACM Transactions on Asian Language Information Processing (TALIP)*, 9(4), pages 4:1–4:21, 2010. DOI: 10.1145/1731035.1731039. 47

Satanjeev Banerjee and Ted Pedersen. An Adapted Lesk Algorithm for Word Sense Disambiguation Using WordNet. In *Computational Linguistics and Intelligent Text Processing (CICLing), 3rd International Conference*, pages 136–145, Mexico City, 2002. DOI: 10.1007/3-540-45715-1_11. 47

Michele Banko, Michael J. Cafarella, Stephen Soderland, Matt Broadhead, and Oren Etzioni. Open Information Extraction from the Web. In *Proc. of the 20th International Joint Conference on Artificial Intelligence (IJCAI)*, pages 2670–2676, Hyderabad, India, 2007. DOI: 10.1145/1409360.1409378. 56, 70

Daniel Bär, Torsten Zesch, and Iryna Gurevych. Text Reuse Detection Using a Composition of Text Similarity Measures. In *Proc. of the 24th International Conference on Computational Linguistics*, pages 167–184, Mumbay, India, 2012. 67

Daniel Bär, Torsten Zesch, and Iryna Gurevych. DKPro Similarity: An Open Source Framework for Text Similarity. In *Proc. of the 51st Conference of the Association for Computational Linguistics*, pages 121–126, Sofia, Bulgaria, 2013. 87

Marco Baroni, Silvia Bernardini, Adriano Ferraresi, and Eros Zanchetta. The WaCky Wide Web: A Collection of Very Large Linguistically Processed Web-Crawled Corpora. *Language Resources and Evaluation*, 43(3), pages 209–226, 2009. DOI: 10.1007/s10579-009-9081-4. 57

Valerio Basile, Johan Bos, Kilian Evang, and Noortje Venhuizen. A Platform for Collaborative Semantic Annotation. In *Proc. of the 13th Conference of the European Chapter of the Association for Computational Linguistics (EACL)*, pages 92–96, Avignon, France, 2012. 80

Valerio Basile, Johan Bos, Kilian Evang, and Noortje Venhuizen. Developing a Large Semantically Annotated Corpus. In *Proc. of the Eighth International Conference on Language Resources and Evaluation (LREC 2012)*, pages 3196–3200, Istanbul, Turkey, 2012. 53

Yoshua Bengio, Réjean Ducharme, Pascal Vincent, and Christian Janvin. A Neural Probabilistic Language Model. *Journal of Machine Learning Research*, 3, pages 1137–1155, 2003. DOI: 10.1007/3-540-33486-6_6. 60

Luisa Bentivogli, Pamela Forner, Bernardo Magnini, and Emanuele Pianta.   Revising the WordNet Domains Hierarchy: Semantics, Coverage and Balancing. In *Proc. of the Workshop on Multilingual Linguistic Ressources*, pages 101–108, Geneva, Switzerland, 2004. DOI: 10.3115/1706238.1706254. 5

Jacob Berlin and Amihai Motro. Database Schema Matching Using Machine Learning with Feature Selection. In *Proc. of the 14th International Conference on Advanced Information Systems Engineering*, pages 452–466, Springer, Toronto, Ontario, Canada, London, UK, 2002. DOI: 10.1007/3-540-47961-9_32. 31

Tim Berners-Lee, James Hendler, and Ora Lassila. The Semantic Web. *Scientific American*, 284(5), pages 34–43, 2001. DOI: 10.1038/scientificamerican0501-34. 19

Sumit Bhagwani, Shrutiranjan Satapathy, and Harish Karnick. Merging Word Senses. In *Proc. of the 8th Workshop on Graph-Based Methods for Natural Language Processing (TextGraphs-8)*, pages 11–19, Seattle, WA, 2013. 52

Eckhard Bick. A FrameNet for Danish. In Bolette Sandford Pedersen, Gunta Nešpore, and Inguna Skadina, Eds., *Proc. of the 18th Nordic Conference of Computational Linguistics*, pages 34–41, Riga, Latvia, 2011. 7

Chris Biemann and Valerie Nygaard. Crowdsourcing WordNet. In *The 5th International Conference of the Global WordNet Association (GWC-2010)*, Mumbai, India, 2010. 80

Chris Biemann and Martin Riedl. Text: Now in 2d! A Framework for Lexical Expansion with Contextual Similarity. *Journal of Language Modelling*, 1(1), pages 55–95, 2013. DOI: 10.15398/jlm.v1i1.60. 47

Christian Bizer, Jens Lehmann, Georgi Kobilarov, Sören Auer, Christian Becker, Richard Cyganiak, and Sebastian Hellmann. DBpedia—A Crystallization Point for the Web of Data. *Journal of Web Semantics: Science, Services and Agents on the World Wide Web*, (7), pages 154–165, 2009. DOI: 10.1016/j.websem.2009.07.002. 12, 19

Olivier Bodenreider. The Unified Medical Language System (UMLS): Integrating Biomedical Terminology. *Nucleic Acids Research*, 32(suppl 1), pages D267–D270, 2004. DOI: 10.1093/nar/gkh061. 3

Francis Bond and Ryan Foster. Linking and Extending an Open Multilingual WordNet. In *Proc. of the 51st Conference of the Association for Computational Linguistics*, pages 1352–1362, Sofia, Bulgaria, 2013. xviii, 25, 26, 41, 69

Claire Bonial, Kevin Stowe, and Martha Palmer. Renewing and Revising SemLink. In *Proc. of the 2nd Workshop on Linked Data in Linguistics (LDL-2013): Representing and Linking Lexicons, Terminologies and other Language Data*, pages 9–17, Pisa, Italy, 2013. 27

Antoine Bordes, Jason Weston, Ronan Collobert, and Yoshua Bengio. Learning Structured Embeddings of Knowledge Bases. In *Proc. of the 25th AAAI Conference on Artificial Intelligence*, pages 301–306, San Francisco, CA, 2011. 62

Antoine Bordes, Nicolas Usunier, Alberto Garcia-Duran, Jason Weston, and Oksana Yakhnenko. Translating Embeddings for Modeling Multi-Relational Data. In C. J. C. Burges, L. Bottou, M. Welling, Z. Ghahramani, and K. Q. Weinberger, Eds., *Advances in Neural Information Processing Systems 26*, pages 2787–2795. Curran Associates, Inc., 2013. 62

Lars Borin, Markus Forsberg, and Johan Roxendal. Korp—The Corpus Infrastructure of Språkbanken. In *Proc. of the Eight International Conference on Language Resources and Evaluation (LREC 2012), Istanbul: ELRA*, pages 474–478, Istanbul, Turkey, 2012. 75

Sergey Brin and Lawrence Page. The Anatomy of a Large-Scale Hypertextual Web Search Engine. *Computer Networks and ISDN Systems*, 30(1–7), pages 107–117, 1998. DOI: 10.1016/s0169-7552(98)00110-x. 34

Paul Buitelaar. Reducing Lexical Semantic Complexity with Systematic Polysemous Classes and Underspecification. In *Proc. of the NAACL-ANLP Workshop on Syntactic and Semantic Complexity in Natural Language Processing Systems*, pages 14–19, Seattle, WA, 2000. DOI: 10.3115/1117543.1117546. 51

Razvan Bunescu and Raymond Mooney. Learning to Extract Relations from the Web Using Minimal Supervision. In *Proc. of the 45th Annual Meeting of the Association for Computational Linguistics (ACL)*, pages 576–583, Prague, Czech Republic, 2007. 58

Thomas Burch and Andrea Rapp. Das Wörterbuch-Netz: Verfahren - Methoden - Perspektiven. In *Geschichte im Netz: Praxis, Chancen, Visionen. Beiträge der Tagung .hist 2006*, Historisches Forum 10, Teilband I, pages 607–627. Humboldt-Universität zu Berlin, Berlin, 2007. 75

Aljoscha Burchardt, Katrin Erk, Anette Frank, Andrea Kowalski, Sebastian Padó, and Manfred Pinkal. The SALSA Corpus: A German Corpus Resource for Lexical Semantics. In *Proc. of the 5th International Conference on Language Resources and Evaluation*, pages 969–974, Genoa, Italy, 2006. 7, 53

Anita Burgun and Olivier Bodenreider. Comparing Terms, Concepts and Semantic Classes in WordNet and the Unified Medical Language System. In *Proc. of NAACL Workshop on WordNet and Other Lexical Resources*, pages 77–82, Pittsburgh, PA, 2001. 25

Nicoletta Calzolari, Monica Monachini, and Claudia Soria. Historical Context and Perspectives. In Gil Francopoulo, Ed., *LMF: Lexical Markup Framework*, Computer Engineering and IT, chapter 1, pages 1–18. Wiley-ISTE, London, UK, 2013. DOI: 10.1002/9781118712696. 16

Michael Carl, Martin Kay, and Kristian Jensen. Long-Distance Revisions in Drafting and Post-Editing. *Research in Computing Science—Special Issue: Natural Language Processing and its Applications*, 46, pages 193–204, 2010. 68

Jen Nan Chen and Jason S. Chang. Topical Clustering of MRD Senses Based on Information Retrieval Techniques. *Computational Linguistics*, 24(1), pages 61–95, 1998. 51

Jianpeng Cheng, Dimitri Kartsaklis, and Edward Grefenstette. Investigating the Role or Prior Disambiguation in Deep-Learning Compositional Models of Meaning. In *Learning Semantics Workshop, NIPS 2014*, Montreal, Canada, 2014. 64

Christian Chiarcos, Sebastian Nordhoff, and Sebastian Hellmann. *Linked Data in Linguistics. Representing Language Data and Metadata*. Springer, Heidelberg, 2012. xix

Christian Chiarcos, John McCrae, Philipp Cimiano, and Christiane Fellbaum. *Towards Open Data for Linguistics: Linguistic Linked Data*, pages 7–25. Springer, Berlin/Heidelberg, 2013. DOI: 10.1007/978-3-642-31782-8_2. 19

Timothy Chklovski and Yolanda Gil. Improving the Design of Intelligent Acquisition Interfaces for Collecting World Knowledge from Web Contributors. In *Proc. of the 3rd International Conference on Knowledge Capture*, pages 35–42, Banff, Alberta, Canada, 2005. ACM, New York. DOI: 10.1145/1088622.1088630. 80

Timothy Chklovski and Rada Mihalcea. Building a Sense Tagged Corpus with Open Mind Word Expert. In *Proc. of the SIGLEX/SENSEVAL Workshop on Word Sense Disambiguation: Recent Successes and Future Directions*, pages 116–122, Philadelphia, PA, 2002. DOI: 10.3115/1118675.1118692. 80

Timothy Chklovski and Rada Mihalcea. Exploiting Agreement and Disagreement of Human Annotators for Word Sense Disambiguation. In *Proc. of the International Conference on Recent Advances in Natural Language Processing*, pages 105–112, Borovets, Bulgaria, 2003. 51

Kostadin Cholakov, Judith Eckle-Kohler, and Iryna Gurevych. Automated Verb Sense Labelling Based on Linked Lexical Resources. In *Proc. of the 14th Conference of the European Chapter of the Association for Computational Linguistics (EACL)*, pages 68–77, Gothenburg, Sweden, 2014. DOI: 10.3115/v1/e14-1008. 23, 57, 59

Ian C. Chow and Jonathan J. Webster. Integration of Linguistic Resources for Verb Classification: FrameNet Frame WordNet Verb and Suggested Upper Merged Ontology. In *Computational Linguistics and Intelligent Text Processing (CICLing), 8th International Conference*, pages 1–11, Mexico City, 2007. DOI: 10.1007/978-3-540-70939-8_1. 22

William Cohen, Pradeep Ravikumar, and Stephen Fienberg. A Comparison of String Metrics for Matching Names and Records. In *Proc. of the KDD-03 Workshop on Data Cleaning, Record Linkage, and Object Consolidation*, pages 73–78, Washington DC, 2003. 30

Ann Copestake and Dan Flickinger. An Open Source Grammar Development Environment and Broad-Coverage English Grammar Using HPSG. In *Proc. of the 2nd International Conference on Language Resources and Evaluation*, pages 591–598, Athens, Greece, 2000. 7

Jim Cowie, Joe Guthrie, and Louise Guthrie. Lexical Disambiguation Using Simulated Annealing. In *Proc. of the 15th International Conference on Computational Linguistics*, pages 359–365, Nantes, France, 1992. DOI: 10.3115/992066.992125. 47

Johannes Daxenberger and Iryna Gurevych. Automatically Classifying Edit Categories in Wikipedia Revisions. In *Joint Conference on Empirical Methods in Natural Language Processing and Computational Natural Language Learning*, pages 578–589, Seattle, WA, 2013. 81

Johannes Daxenberger, Oliver Ferschke, and Iryna Gurevych. Wikipedia-Based Corpora for Analyzing Revisions, Discussions and Text Quality in Collaborative Writing. *Workshop on Automatic Processing of Non-Standard Data Sources in Corpus-Based Research*, (Extended Abstract), Cologne, Germany, 2012. 81

Gerard De Melo and Gerhard Weikum. A Machine Learning Approach to Building Aligned WordNets. In *Proc. of the First International Conference on Global Interoperability for Language Resources*, pages 163–170, Hong Kong, 2008. 26, 41

Gerard De Melo and Gerhard Weikum. Towards a Universal WordNet by Learning from Combined Evidence. In *Proc. of the ACM 19th Conference on Information and Knowledge Management (CIKM 2010)*, pages 513–522, Hong Kong, 2009. DOI: 10.1145/1645953.1646020. 26

Gerard de Melo and Gerhard Weikum. MENTA: Inducing Multilingual Taxonomies from Wikipedia. In *Proc. of the 19th ACM International Conference on Information and Knowledge Management*, pages 1099–1108, Toronto, ON, Canada, 2010. DOI: 10.1145/1871437.1871577. 12

Gerard De Melo and Gerhard Weikum. Providing Multilingual, Multimodal Answers to Lexical Database Queries. In *Proc. of the 7th International Conference on Language Resources and Evaluation (LREC)*, pages 348–355, La Valetta, Malta, 2010. 25, 26

Bart Decadt, Véronique Hoste, Walter Daelemans, and Antal van den Bosch. GAMBL, Genetic Algorithm Optimization of Memory-Based WSD. In *Proc. of the 3rd International Workshop on the Evaluation of Systems for the Semantic Analysis of Text (SENSEVAL-3) at ACL-04*, pages 108–112, Barcelona, Spain, 2004. 47

Thierry Declerck, Karlheinz Mörth, and Piroska Lendvai. Accessing and Standardizing Wiktionary Lexical Entries for the Translation of Labels in Cultural Heritage Taxonomies. In *Proc. of the 8th International Conference on Language Resources and Evaluation (LREC 2012)*, pages 2511–2514, Istanbul, Turkey, 2012. 69

Scott Deerwester, Susan T. Dumais, George W. Furnas, Thomas K. Landauer, and Richard Harshman. Indexing by Latent Semantic Analysis. *Journal of the American Society for Information Science*, 41(6), pages 391–407, 1990. DOI: 10.1002/(sici)1097-4571(199009)41:6%3C391::aid-asi1%3E3.0.co;2-9. 87

Riccardo Del Gratta, Francesca Frontini, Anas Fahad Khan, and Monica Monachini. Converting the PAROLE SIMPLE CLIPS Lexicon into RDF with Lemon. *Semantic Web*, 6(4), pages 387–392, 2015. DOI: 10.3233/sw-140168. 19

Robin Dhamankar, Yoonkyong Lee, Anhai Doan, Alon Halevy, and Pedro Domingos. iMAP: Discovering Complex Semantic Matches Between Database Schemas. In *Proc. of the 2004 ACM SIGMOD International Conference on Management of Data*, pages 383–394, Paris, France, 2004. DOI: 10.1145/1007568.1007612. 30

Edsger W. Dijkstra. A Note on Two Problems in Connexion with Graphs. *Numerische Mathematik*, 1, pages 269–271, 1959. DOI: 10.1007/bf01386390. 39

Anhai Doan, Jayant Madhavan, Pedro Domingos, and Alon Halevy. Ontology Matching: A Machine Learning Approach. In *Handbook on Ontologies in Information Systems*, pages 397–416, Springer, 2003. DOI: 10.1007/978-3-540-24750-0_19. 30

William B. Dolan. Word Sense Ambiguation: Clustering Related Senses. In *Proc. of the 15th International Conference on Computational Linguistics*, pages 712–716, Kyoto, Japan, 1994. DOI: 10.3115/991250.991260. 51

Xin Dong, Evgeniy Gabrilovich, Geremy Heitz, Wilko Horn, Ni Lao, Kevin Murphy, Thomas Strohmann, Shaohua Sun, and Wei Zhang. Knowledge Vault: A Web-Scale Approach to Probabilistic Knowledge Fusion. In *Proc. of the 20th ACM SIGKDD International Conference on Knowledge Discovery and Data Mining*, pages 601–610, New York, NY, 2014. DOI: 10.1145/2623330.2623623. 56

Richard Eckart de Castilho, Sabine Bartsch, and Iryna Gurevych. CSniper—Annotation-by-Query for Non-Canonical Constructions in Large Corpora. In *Proc. of the ACL 2012 System Demonstrations*, pages 85–90, Jeju Island, Korea, 2012. 80

Judith Eckle-Kohler. *Linguistisches Wissen zur Automatischen Lexikon-Akquisition aus Deutschen Textcorpora*. Logos-Verlag, Berlin, Germany, 1999. Ph.D. Thesis. 9

Judith Eckle-Kohler and Iryna Gurevych. Subcat-LMF: Fleshing out a Standardized Format for Subcategorization Frame Interoperability Across Languages. In *Proc. of the 13th Conference of the European Chapter of the Association for Computational Linguistics (EACL)*, pages 550–560, Avignon, France, 2012. 8, 18

Judith Eckle-Kohler, Iryna Gurevych, Silvana Hartmann, Michael Matuschek, and Christian M. Meyer. UBY-LMF—A Uniform Model for Standardizing Heterogeneous Lexical-Semantic Resources in ISO-LMF. In *Proc. of the 8th International Conference on Language Resources and Evaluation (LREC 2012)*, pages 275–282, Istanbul, Turkey, 2012. 18

Judith Eckle-Kohler, Iryna Gurevych, Silvana Hartmann, Michael Matuschek, and Christian M. Meyer. UBY-LMF—Exploring the Boundaries of Language-Independent Lexicon Models. In Gil Francopoulo, Ed., *LMF: Lexical Markup Framework*, Computer Engineering and IT, chapter 10, pages 145–156. Wiley-ISTE, London, 2013. DOI: 10.1002/9781118712696. 18

Judith Eckle-Kohler, Daniela Oelke, and Iryna Gurevych. Visualization Design for a Web Interface to the Large-Scale Linked Lexical Resource Uby. *Abstract Herrenhäuser Symposium: Visual Linguistics. Theory and Application of Visualization in Linguistics*, 2014. 78

Judith Eckle-Kohler, John Philip McCrae, and Christian Chiarcos. LemonUby—A Large, Interlinked, Syntactically-Rich Lexical Resource for Ontologies. *Semantic Web Journal*, vol. 6, no. 4, pages 371–378, 2015. DOI: 10.3233/sw-140159. 83

Stefan Engelberg and Lothar Lemnitzer, Eds. *Lexikographie und Wörterbuchbenutzung*, vol. 14 of *Einführungen*. Stauffenburg, Tübingen, 2001. 37

Soojeong Eom, Markus Dickinson, and Graham Katz. Using Semi-Experts to Derive Judgments on Word Sense Alignment: A Pilot Study. In *Proc. of the 8th International Conference on Language Resources and Evaluation (LREC 2012)*, pages 605–611, Istanbul, Turkey, 2012. 80

Nicolai Erbs, Torsten Zesch, and Iryna Gurevych. Link Discovery: A Comprehensive Analysis. In *Proc. of the 5th IEEE International Conference on Semantic Computing*, pages 83–86, Stanford University, Palo Alto, CA, 2011. DOI: 10.1109/icsc.2011.63. 46

Nicolai Erbs, Iryna Gurevych, and Torsten Zesch. Sense and Similarity: A Study of Sense-Level Similarity Measures. In *Proc. of the 3rd Joint Conference on Lexical and Computational Semantics (*SEM 2014)*, pages 30–39, Dublin, Ireland, 2014. DOI: 10.3115/v1/s14-1004. 67

Maike Erdmann, Kotaro Nakayama, Takahiro Hara, and Shojiro Nishio. An Approach for Extracting Bilingual Terminology from Wikipedia. In *Database Systems for Advanced Applications*, vol. 4947 of *Lecture Notes in Computer Science*, pages 380–392. Springer, Berlin/Heidelberg, 2009. DOI: 10.1007/978-3-540-78568-2_28. 12, 70

Jérôme Euzenat and Pavel Shvaiko. *Ontology Matching*. Springer, Heidelberg, Germany, 2nd ed., 2013. DOI: 10.1007/978-3-642-38721-0. 29

Manaal Faruqui, Jesse Dodge, Sujay Kumar Jauhar, Chris Dyer, Eduard Hovy, and Noah A. Smith. Retrofitting Word Vectors to Semantic Lexicons. In *Proc. of the 2015 Conference of the North American Chapter of the Association for Computational Linguistics: Human Language Technologies (NAACL-HLT)*, pages 1606–1615, Denver, CO, 2015. DOI: 10.3115/v1/n15-1184. 64

Christiane Fellbaum, Ed. *WordNet: An Electronic Lexical Database*. MIT Press, Cambridge, MA, 1998. DOI: 10.1093/oxfordhb/9780199842193.013.001. xiii, xviii, 4, 50

Oscar Ferrandez, Michael Ellsworth, Rafael Munoz, and Collin F. Baker. Aligning FrameNet and WordNet Based on Semantic Neighborhoods. In *Proc. of the 7th International Conference on Language Resources and Evaluation (LREC)*, pages 310–314, La Valetta, Malta, 2010. 26, 40

Charles J. Fillmore. Frame Semantics. In *Linguistics in the Morning Calm*, pages 111–137. Linguistic Society of Korea, Hanshin Publishing Company, 1982. DOI: 10.1016/b0-08-044854-2/00424-7. 6

Arne Fitschen. *Ein Computerlinguistisches Lexikon als Komplexes System*. Ph.D. Thesis, Universität Stuttgart, Stuttgart, Germany, 2004. 9

Tiziano Flati and Roberto Navigli. The CQC Algorithm: Cycling in Graphs to Semantically Enrich and Enhance a Bilingual Dictionary. *Journal of Artificial Intelligence Research (JAIR)*, 43, pages 135–171, 2012. 39

Tiziano Flati and Roberto Navigli. SPred: Large-Scale Harvesting of Semantic Predicates. In *Proc. of the 51st Conference of the Association for Computational Linguistics*, pages 1222–1232, Sofia, Bulgaria, 2013. 24, 48

Lucie Flekova and Iryna Gurevych. Personality Profiling of Fictional Characters Using Sense-Level Links Between Lexical Resources. In *Proc. of the 2015 Conference on Empirical Methods in Natural Language Processing*, pages 1805–1816, Lisbon, Portugal, 2015. DOI: 10.18653/v1/d15-1208. 50

Marco Fossati, Claudio Giuliano, and Sara Tonelli. Outsourcing FrameNet to the Crowd. In *Proc. of the 51st Conference of the Association for Computational Linguistics*, pages 742–747, Sofia, Bulgaria, 2013. 80

Gil Francopoulo and Monte George. Model Description. In Gil Francopoulo, Ed., *LMF: Lexical Markup Framework*, chapter 2, pages 19–40. Wiley-ISTE, London, 2013. DOI: 10.1002/9781118712696. 16

Gil Francopoulo, Nuria Bel, Monte George, Nicoletta Calzolari, Monica Monachini, Mandy Pet, and Claudia Soria. Multilingual Resources for NLP in the Lexical Markup Framework (LMF). *Language Resources and Evaluation*, 43(1), pages 57–70, 2009. DOI: 10.1007/s10579-008-9077-5. 23

Karin Friberg Heppin and Maria Toporowska Gronostaj. The Rocky Road Towards a Swedish FrameNet—Creating SweFN. In *Proc. of the 8th International Conference on Language Resources and Evaluation (LREC 2012)*, pages 256–261, Istanbul, Turkey, 2012. 7

Sanae Fujita and Akinori Fujino. Word Sense Disambiguation by Combining Labeled Data Expansion and Semi-Supervised Learning Method. In *Proc. of the 5th International Joint Conference on Natural Language Processing*, pages 676–685, Chiang Mai, Thailand, 2011. DOI: 10.1145/2461316.2461319. 48

Benoît Gaillard, Malek Boualem, and Olivier Collin. Query Translation Using Wikipedia-Based Resources for Analysis and Disambiguation. In *Proc. of the 14th Annual Conference of the European Association for Machine Translation (EAMT 2010)*, Saint-Raphael, France, 2010. 70

Luis A. Galárraga, Nicoleta Preda, and Fabian M. Suchanek. Mining Rules to Align Knowledge Bases. In *Proc. of the 2013 Workshop on Automated Knowledge Base Construction*, pages 43–48, San Francisco, CA, 2013. DOI: 10.1145/2509558.2509566. 56

Juri Ganitkevitch, Benjamin Van Durme, and Chris Callison-Burch. PPDB: The Paraphrase Database. In *Proc. of the Human Language Technology Conference of the North American Chapter of the Association for Computational Linguistics*, page 758–764, Atlanta, GA, 2013. 64

Konstantina Garoufi, Torsten Zesch, and Iryna Gurevych. Graph-Theoretic Analysis of Collaborative Knowledge Bases in Natural Language Processing. In *Proc. of the 7th International Semantic Web Conference*, pages 48–49, Karlsruhe, Germany, 2008. 37

Jim Giles. Internet Encyclopaedias Go Head to Head. *Nature*, 438(7070), pages 900–901, 2005. DOI: 10.1038/438900a. xvii, 11

Fausto Giunchiglia, Pavel Shvaiko, and Mikalai Yatskevich. S-Match: An Algorithm and an Implementation of Semantic Matching. In Christoph J. Bussler, John Davies, Dieter Fensel, and Rudi Studer, Eds., *The Semantic Web: Research and Applications*, vol. 3053 of *Lecture Notes in Computer Science*, pages 61–75. Springer, Berlin/Heidelberg, 2004. DOI: 10.1007/b97867. 30

Ralph Grishman, Catherine Macleod, and Adam Meyers. Comlex Syntax: Building a Computational Lexicon. In *Proc. of the 15th International Conference on Computational Linguistics*, pages 268–272, Kyoto, Japan, 1994. DOI: 10.3115/991886.991931. 8

Shu Guo, Quan Wang, Bin Wang, Lihong Wang, and Li Guo. Semantically Smooth Knowledge Graph Embedding. In *Proc. of the 53rd Annual Meeting of the Association for Computational Linguistics and the 7th International Joint Conference on Natural Language Processing*, pages 84–94, Beijing, China, 2015. DOI: 10.3115/v1/p15-1009. 61, 62

Iryna Gurevych and Jungi Kim, Eds. *The People's Web Meets NLP: Collaboratively Constructed Language Resources*. Theory and Applications of Natural Language Processing. Springer, Berlin/Heidelberg, 2012. 12

Iryna Gurevych and Elisabeth Wolf. Expert-Built and Collaboratively Constructed Lexical-Semantic Resources. *Language and Linguistics Compass*, 4(11), pages 1074–1090, 2010. DOI: 10.1111/j.1749-818x.2010.00251.x. 13

Iryna Gurevych, Judith Eckle-Kohler, Silvana Hartmann, Michael Matuschek, Christian M. Meyer, and Christian Wirth. UBY—A Large-Scale Unified Lexical-Semantic Resource Based on LMF. In *Proc. of the 13th Conference of the European Chapter of the Association for Computational Linguistics (EACL)*, pages 580–590, Avignon, France, 2012. 23, 36

Iryna Gurevych, Michael Matuschek, Tri-Duc Nghiem, Judith Eckle-Kohler, Silvana Hartmann, and Christian M. Meyer. Navigating Sense-Aligned Lexical-Semantic Resources: The Web Interface to UBY. In *Proc. of the 11th "Konferenz zur Verarbeitung natürlicher Sprache" (KONVENS 2012)*, pages 194–198, Vienna, Austria, 2012b. 77

Kelvin Guu, John Miller, and Percy Liang. Traversing Knowledge Graphs in Vector Space. In *Proc. of the 2015 Conference on Empirical Methods in Natural Language Processing*, pages 318–327, Lisbon, Portugal, 2015. DOI: 10.18653/v1/d15-1038. 62

102   BIBLIOGRAPHY

Mark Hall, Frank Eibe, Geoffrey Holmes, Bernhard Pfahringer, Peter Reutemann, and Ian H. Witten. The WEKA Data Mining Software: An Update. *SIGKDD Explorations*, 11(1), pages 10–18, 2009. DOI: 10.1145/1656274.1656278. 41

Birgit Hamp and Helmut Feldweg. GermaNet—A Lexical-Semantic Net for German. In *Proc. of the ACL Workshop on Automatic Information Extraction and Building of Lexical Semantic Resources for NLP Applications*, pages 9–15, Madrid, Spain, 1997. 5, 50

Silvana Hartmann and Iryna Gurevych. FrameNet on the Way to Babel: Creating a Bilingual FrameNet Using Wiktionary as Interlingual Connection. In *Proc. of the 51st Conference of the Association for Computational Linguistics*, vol. 1, pages 1363–1373, Sofia, Bulgaria, 2013. 35

Silvana Hartmann, Judith Eckle-Kohler, and Iryna Gurevych. Generating Training Data for Semantic Role Labeling Based on Label Transfer from Linked Lexical Resources. *Transactions of the Association for Computational Linguistics*, vol. 4, pages 197–213, May 2016. 59

Joshua K. Hartshorne, Claire Bonial, and Martha Palmer. The VerbCorner Project: Findings from Phase 1 of Crowd-Sourcing a Semantic Decomposition of Verbs. In *Proc. of the 52nd Conference of the Association for Computational Linguistics*, pages 397–402, Baltimore, MD, 2014. DOI: 10.3115/v1/p14-2065. 9

Verena Henrich and Erhard Hinrichs. Standardizing WordNets in the ISO Standard LMF: WordNet-LMF for GermaNet. In *Proc. of the 23rd International Conference on Computational Linguistics (COLING)*, pages 456–464, Beijing, China, 2010. 18

Verena Henrich and Erhard Hinrichs. A Comparative Evaluation of Word Sense Disambiguation Algorithms for German. In *Proc. of the 8th International Conference on Language Resources and Evaluation (LREC 2012)*, pages 576–583, Istanbul, Turkey, 2012. 47, 50

Verena Henrich, Erhard Hinrichs, and Tatiana Vodolazova. Semi-Automatic Extension of GermaNet with Sense Definitions from Wiktionary. In *Proc. of the 5th Language and Technology Conference*, pages 126–130, Poznan, Poland, 2011. 25, 26, 35

Verena Henrich, Erhard Hinrichs, and Tatiana Vodolazova. WebCAGe—A Web-Harvested Corpus Annotated with GermaNet Senses. In *Proc. of the 13th Conference of the European Chapter of the Association for Computational Linguistics (EACL)*, pages 387–396, Avignon, France, 2012. 53

Benjamin Herbert, György Szarvas, and Iryna Gurevych. Combining Query Translation Techniques to Improve Cross-Language Information Retrieval. *Lecture Notes in Computer Science*, vol. 6611, pages 712–715, Springer, Berlin/Heidelberg, 2011. DOI: 10.1007/978-3-642-20161-5_77. 70

Karl Moritz Hermann, Dipanjan Das, Jason Weston, and Kuzman Ganchev. Semantic Frame Identification with Distributed Word Representations. In *Proc. of the 52nd Conference of the Association for Computational Linguistics*, pages 1448–1458, Baltimore, MD, 2014. DOI: 10.3115/v1/p14-1136. 65

Barbora Hladká, Jiří Mírovský, and Pavel Schlesinger. Play the Language: Play Coreference. In *Proc. of the Joint Conference of the 47th Annual Meeting of the Association for Computational Linguistics and the 4th International Joint Conference on Natural Language Processing*, pages 209–212, Singapore, 2009. DOI: 10.3115/1667583.1667648. 80

Raphael Hoffmann, Congle Zhang, Xiao Ling, Luke Zettlemoyer, and Daniel S. Weld. Knowledge-Based Weak Supervision for Information Extraction of Overlapping Relations. In *Proc. of the 49th Annual Meeting of the Association for Computational Linguistics (ACL)*, pages 541–550, Portland, Oreg., 2011. 59

Aleš Horák and Pavel Smrž. VisDic—Wordnet Browsing and Editing Tool. In *Proc. of GWC 2004*, pages 136–141, Brno, Czech Republic, 2004. 75

Malka Rappaport Hovav and Beth Levin. The English Dative Alternation: The Case for Verb Sensitivity. *Journal of Linguistics*, 44, pages 129–167, 2008. DOI: 10.1017/s0022226707004975. 8

Eduard Hovy, Mitchell Marcus, Martha Palmer, Lance Ramshaw, and Ralph Weischedel. OntoNotes: The 90% Solution. In *Proc. of the Human Language Technology Conference of the North American Chapter of the Association for Computational Linguistics*, pages 57–60, New York, 2006. 53

Ignacio Iacobacci, Mohammad Taher Pilehvar, and Roberto Navigli. SensEmbed: Learning Sense Embeddings for Word and Relational Similarity. In *Proc. of the 53rd Annual Meeting of the Association for Computational Linguistics and the 7th International Joint Conference on Natural Language Processing*, pages 95–105, Beijing, China, 2015. DOI: 10.3115/v1/p15-1010. 64, 65

Nancy Ide. Making Senses: Bootstrapping Sense-Tagged Lists of Semantically-Related Words. In *Computational Linguistics and Intelligent Text Processing (CICLing), 7th International Conference*, Mexico City, 2006, *Lecture Notes in Computer Science*, vol. 387 pages 13–27, Springer, Berlin/Heidelberg, 2006. DOI: 10.1007/11671299_2. 51

Nancy Ide and James Pustejovsky. What Does Interoperability Mean, Anyway? Toward an Operational Definition of Interoperability. In *Proc. of the 2nd International Conference on Global Interoperability for Language Resources*, Hong Kong, 2010. 18

Nancy Ide and Yorick Wilks. Making Sense About Sense. In Eneko Agirre and Philip Edmonds, Eds., *Word Sense Disambiguation: Algorithms and Applications*, vol. 33 of *Text, Speech, and Language Technology*, chapter 3. Springer, 2006. DOI: 10.1007/978-1-4020-4809-8. 51

Ryu Iida, Diana McCarthy, and Rob Koeling. Gloss-Based Semantic Similarity Metrics for Predominant Sense Acquisition. In *Proc. of the 3rd International Joint Conference on Natural Language Processing*, pages 561–568, Hyderabad, India, 2008. 47

Hitoshi Isahara, Fransis Bond, Kiyotaka Uchimoto, Masao Utiyama, and Kyoko Kanzaki. Development of the Japanese WordNet. In *Proc. of the 6th International Conference on Language Resources and Evaluation (LREC)*, pages 2420–2423, Marrakech, Morocco, 2008. 5

ISO12620. *Terminology and Other Language and Content Resources—Specification of Data Categories and Management of a Data Category Registry for Language Resources.* Number ISO 12620:2009. International Organization for Standardization, Geneva, Switzerland, 2009. DOI: 10.3403/30138758. 17

ISO24613. *Language Resource Management—Lexical Markup Framework (LMF).* Number ISO 24613:2008. International Organization for Standardization, Geneva, Switzerland, 2008. DOI: 10.3403/30138761. 16

Peter Jansen. Lexicography in an Interlingual Ontology: An Introduction to EuroWordNet. *Canadian Undergraduate Journal of Cognitive Science*, 3, pages 1–5, 2004. 26

Guoliang Ji, Shizhu He, Liheng Xu, Kang Liu, and Jun Zhao. Knowledge Graph Embedding via Dynamic Mapping Matrix. In *Proc. of the 53rd Annual Meeting of the Association for Computational Linguistics and the 7th International Joint Conference on Natural Language Processing*, pages 687–696, Beijing, China, 2015. DOI: 10.3115/v1/p15-1067. 62

Hongyan Jing and Kathleen McKeown. Combining Multiple, Large-Scale Resources in a Reusable Lexicon for Natural Language Generation. In *Proc. of the 17th International Conference on Computational Linguistics and 36th Annual Meeting of the Association for Computational Linguistics*, pages 607–613, Montréal, Québec, Canada, 1998. DOI: 10.3115/980451.980946. 22

Richard Johansson and Pierre Nugues. Using WordNet to Extend FrameNet Coverage. In *Building Frame Semantics Resources for Scandinavian and Baltic Languages*, pages 27–30. Department of Computer Science, Lund University, 2007. 26

David Jürgens and Ioannis Klapaftis. SemEval-2013 Task 13: Word Sense Induction for Graded and Non-Graded Senses. In *Proc. of the 5th International Workshop on Semantic Evaluation collocated with the Second Joint Conference on Lexical and Computational Semantics*, pages 290–299, Atlanta, GA, 2013. 48

David Jürgens, Saif Mohammad, Peter Turney, and Keith Holyoak. SemEval-2012 Task 2: Measuring Degrees of Relational Similarity. In *SEM 2012: The First Joint Conference on Lexical and Computational Semantics—Volume 1: Proc. of the Main Conference and the Shared Task, and Volume 2: Proc. of the 6th International Workshop on Semantic Evaluation (SemEval 2012)*, pages 356–364, Montréal, Canada, 2012. 64

Jaewoo Kang and Jeffrey F. Naughton. On Schema Matching with Opaque Column Names and Data Values. In *Proc. of the 2003 ACM SIGMOD International Conference on Management of Data*, pages 205–216, San Diego, CA, 2003. DOI: 10.1145/872757.872783. 31

Aida Khemakhem, Bilel Gargouri, Kais Haddar, and Abdelmajid Ben Hamadou. LMF for Arabic. In Gil Francopoulo, Ed., *LMF: Lexical Markup Framework*, Computer Engineering and IT, chapter 6, pages 83–98. Wiley-ISTE, London, 2013. DOI: 10.1002/9781118712696. 18

Adam Kilgarriff. A Detailed, Accurate, Extensive, Available English Lexical Database. In *Proc. of Human Language Technologies 2010: The Conference of the North American Chapter of the Association for Computational Linguistics (NAACL-HLT)*, pages 21–24, Los Angeles, CA., 2010. 3, 75

Tracy Holloway King and Dick Crouch. Unifying Lexical Resources. In Katrin Erk, Alissa Melinger, and Sabine Schulte im Walde, Eds., *Proc. of the Interdisciplinary Workshop on the Identification and Representation of Verb Features and Verb Classes*, pages 32–37, Saarbruecken, Germany, 2005. 22

Karin Kipper, Anna Korhonen, Neville Ryant, and Martha Palmer. Extending VerbNet with Novel Verb Classes. In *Proc. of the 5th International Conference on Language Resources and Evaluation*, pages 1027–1032, Genoa, Italy, 2006. 9

Karin Kipper, Anna Korhonen, Neville Ryant, and Martha Palmer. A Large-Scale Classification of English Verbs. *Language Resources and Evaluation*, 42, pages 21–40, 2008. DOI: 10.1007/s10579-007-9048-2. 9

Christian Kirschner. Kombination Mehrerer Lexikalisch-Semantischer Ressourcen durch Multiple Alignments von Wortbedeutungen. Master thesis, Technische Universtität Darmstadt, 2012. 23

Wolfgang Klein and Alexander Geyken. Das Digitale Wörterbuch der Deutschen Sprache (DWDS). *Lexicographica*, 26, pages 79–96, 2010. 3, 75

Kevin Knight and Steve K. Luk. Building a Large-Scale Knowledge Base for Machine Translation. In *Proc. of the 12th National Conference on Artificial Intelligence*, pages 773–778, Seattle, WA, 1994. 22

Philipp Koehn. A Process Study of Computer Aided Translation. *Machine Translation*, 23(4), pages 241–263, 2009. DOI: 10.1007/s10590-010-9076-3. 68

Upali Sathyajith Kohomban and Wee Sun Lee. Learning Semantic Classes for Word Sense Disambiguation. In *Proc. of the 43rd Annual Meeting of the Association for Computational Linguistics (ACL)*, pages 34–41, Ann Arbor, MI, 2005. DOI: 10.3115/1219840.1219845. 51

Anna Korhonen and Ted Briscoe. Extended Lexical-Semantic Classification of English Verbs. In *Proc. of the HLT-NAACL Workshop on Computational Lexical Semantics*, pages 38–45, Boston, MA, 2004. DOI: 10.3115/1596431.1596437. 9

Sebastian Krause, Hong Li, Hans Uszkoreit, and Feiyu Xu. Large-Scale Learning of Relation-Extraction Rules with Distant Supervision from the Web. In *Proc. of the 11th International Semantic Web Conference*, pages 263–278, Springer, Berlin/Heidelberg, 2012. DOI: 10.1007/978-3-642-35176-1_17. 59

Andrew Krizhanovsky. A Quantitative Analysis of the English Lexicon in Wiktionaries and WordNet. *International Journal of Intelligent Information Technologies*, 8(4), pages 13–22, 2012. DOI: 10.4018/jiit.2012100102. 13

Claudia Kunze and Lothar Lemnitzer. GermaNet—Representation, Visualization, Application. In *Proc. of the 3rd International Conference on Language Resources and Evaluation*, pages 1485–1491, Las Palmas, Canary Islands, Spain, 2002. 75

Oi Yee Kwong. Aligning WordNet with Additional Lexical Resources. In *Proc. of the COLING-ACL'98 Workshop "Usage of WordNet in Natural Language Processing Systems"*, pages 73–79, Montreal, Canada, 1998. 25

Mathieu Lafourcade and Alain Joubert. Computing Trees of Named Word Usages from a Crowdsourced Lexical Network. In *Proc. of the 2010 International Multiconference on Computer Science and Information Technology (IMCSIT)*, pages 439–446, Wisla, Poland, 2010. DOI: 10.1109/imcsit.2010.5680051. 80

Egoitz Laparra and German Rigau. Integrating WordNet and FrameNet Using a Knowledge-Based Word Sense Disambiguation Algorithm. In *Proc. of the International Conference on Recent Advances in Natural Language Processing*, pages 208–213, Borovets, Bulgaria, 2009. 26

Egoitz Laparra, German Rigau, and Montse Cuadros. Exploring the Integration of WordNet and FrameNet. In *Proc. of the 5th International Global WordNet Conference*, Mumbai, India, 2010. 26, 38, 39, 87

Bach Thanh Le, Rose Dieng-Kuntz, and Fabien Gandon. On Ontology Matching Problems—for Building a Corporate Semantic Web in a Multi-Communities Organization. In *Proc. of the 4th International Conference on Enterprise Information Systems (ICEIS 2004)*, pages 236–243, Porto, Portugal, 2004. DOI: 10.5220/0002642802360243. 30

Lung-Hao Lee, Shu-Kai Hsieh, and Chu-Ren Huang. CWN-LMF: Chinese WordNet in the Lexical Markup Framework. In *Proc. of the 7th Workshop on Asian Language Resources*, pages 123–130, Suntec, Singapore, 2009. DOI: 10.3115/1690299.1690317. 18

Michael Lesk. Automatic Sense Disambiguation Using Machine Readable Dictionaries: How to Tell a Pine Cone from an Ice Cream Cone. In *Proc. of the 5th Annual International Conference on Systems Documentation (SIGDOC 1986)*, pages 24–26, Toronto, Canada, 1986. DOI: 10.1145/318723.318728. 33, 47

Beth Levin. *English Verb Classes and Alternations*. The University of Chicago Press, Chicago, IL, 1993. 9

Beth Levin. Semantics and Pragmatics of Argument Alternations. *Annual Review of Linguistics*, 1(1), pages 63–83, 2015. DOI: 10.1146/annurev-linguist-030514-125141. 9

Omer Levy and Yoav Goldberg. Neural Word Embedding as Implicit Matrix Factorization. In *Advances in Neural Information Processing Systems 27: Annual Conference on Neural Information Processing Systems*, pages 2177–2185, Montreal, Quebec, Canada, 2014. 60

Omer Levy, Yoav Goldberg, and Ido Dagan. Improving Distributional Similarity with Lessons Learned from Word Embeddings. *Transactions of the Association for Computational Linguistics*, 3, pages 211–225, 2015. 60

Robert Lew. Online Dictionaries of English. In Pedro A. Fuertes-Olivera and Henning Bergenholtz, Eds., *E-Lexicography: The Internet, Digital Initiatives and Lexicography*, pages 230–250. Continuum, London/New York, 2011. DOI: 10.5040/9781474211833. 3, 75

Hong Li, Sebastian Krause, Feiyu Xu, Andrea Moro, Hans Uszkoreit, and Roberto Navigli. Improvement of n-ary Relation Extraction by Adding Lexical Semantics to Distant-Supervision Rule Learning. In *ICAART 2015—Proc. of the 7th International Conference on Agents and Artificial Intelligence*, pages 317–324, SciTePress, 2015. DOI: 10.5220/0005187303170324. 59

Yankai Lin, Zhiyuan Liu, Huanbo Luan, Maosong Sun, Siwei Rao, and Song Liu. Modeling Relation Paths for Representation Learning of Knowledge Bases. In *Proc. of the 2015 Conference on Empirical Methods in Natural Language Processing*, pages 705–714, Lisbon, Portugal, 2015. DOI: 10.18653/v1/d15-1082. 63

Yuanfei Luo, Quan Wang, Bin Wang, and Li Guo. Context-Dependent Knowledge Graph Embedding. In *Proc. of the 2015 Conference on Empirical Methods in Natural Language Processing*, pages 1656–1661, Lisbon, Portugal, 2015. DOI: 10.18653/v1/d15-1191. 62

Catherine Macleod, Adam Meyers, and Ralph Grishman. The Influence of Tagging on the Classification of Lexical Complements. In *Proc. of the 16th International Conference on Computational Linguistics*, pages 472–477, Copenhagen, Denmark, 1996. DOI: 10.3115/992628.992710. 53

Alexander Maedche and Steffen Staab. Measuring Similarity Between Ontologies. In *Knowledge Engineering and Knowledge Management: Ontologies and the Semantic Web*, pages 251–263, Springer, Berlin/Heidelberg, 2002. DOI: 10.1007/3-540-45810-7_24. 30

Suresh Manandhar, Ioannis P. Klapaftis, Dmitriy Dligach, and Sameer S. Pradhan. SemEval-2010 Task 14: Word Sense Induction and Disambiguation. In *Proc. of the 7th International Workshop on Semantic Evaluation*, pages 63–68, Los Angeles, CA, 2010. 48

Christopher D. Manning and Hinrich Schütze. *Foundations of Statistical Natural Language Processing*, MIT Press, Cambridge, MA, 1999. xiii

Christopher D. Manning. Computational Linguistics and Deep Learning. *Computational Linguistics*, 41(4), pages 701–707, 2015. DOI: 10.1162/coli_a_00239. 66

Lluís Màrquez, Gerard Exsudero, David Martínez, and German Rigau. Supervised Corpus-Based Methods for WSD. In Eneko Agirre and Philip Edmonds, Eds., *Word Sense Disambiguation: Algorithms and Applications*, vol. 33 of *Text, Speech and Language Technology*, pages 167–216, Springer, 2006. DOI: 10.1007/978-1-4020-4809-8. 47

Michael Matuschek. *Word Sense Alignment of Lexical Resources*. Dissertation, Technische Universität Darmstadt, 2014. *Creative Commons Attribution Non-commercial No Derivatives.* 23, 27, 37

Michael Matuschek and Iryna Gurevych. Where the Journey is Headed: Collaboratively Constructed Multilingual Wiki-Based Resources. In SFB 538: Mehrsprachigkeit, Ed., *Hamburger Arbeiten zur Mehrsprachigkeit*. Hamburg, Germany, 2011. 15

Michael Matuschek and Iryna Gurevych. Dijkstra-WSA: A Graph-Based Approach to Word Sense Alignment. *Transactions of the Association for Computational Linguistics (TACL)*, 1, pages 151–164, 2013. 39, 40, 41, 52

Michael Matuschek and Iryna Gurevych. High Performance Word Sense Alignment by Joint Modeling of Sense Distance and Gloss Similarity. In *Proc. of the 26th International Conference on Computational Linguistics*, pages 245–256, Dublin, Ireland, 2014. 40

Michael Matuschek, Christian M. Meyer, and Iryna Gurevych. Multilingual Knowledge in Aligned Wiktionary and OmegaWiki for Computer-Aided Translation. *Translation: Computation, Corpora, Cognition. Special Issue on "Language Technology for a Multilingual Europe"*, 3(1), pages 87–118, 2013. xviii, 70, 71, 72

Michael Matuschek, Tristan Miller, and Iryna Gurevych. A Language-Independent Sense Clustering Approach for Enhanced WSD. In Josef Ruppenhoter and Gertrud Faaß, Eds., *Proc. of the 12th Konferenz zur Verarbeitung Natürlicher Sprache*, pages 11–21, Hildesheim, Germany, Universitätsverlag Hildesheim, 2014. 52

Diana McCarthy. Relating WordNet Senses for Word Sense Disambiguation. In *Proc. of the EACL 2006 Workshop on Making Sense of Sense: Bringing Computational Linguistics and Psycholinguistics Together*, pages 17–24, Trento, Italy, 2006. 51

John McCrae, Dennis Spohr, and Philipp Cimiano. Linking Lexical Resources and Ontologies on the Semantic Web with Lemon. In *The Semantic Web: Research and Applications*, vol. 6643 of *Lecture Notes in Computer Science*, pages 245–259, Springer, Berlin/Heidelberg, 2011. DOI: 10.1007/978-3-642-21034-1_17. 19, 83

John McCrae, Guadalupe Aguado-de-Cea, Paul Buitelaar, Philipp Cimiano, Thierry Declerck, Asunción Gómez-Pérez, Jorge Gracia, Laura Hollink, Elena Montiel-Ponsoda, Dennis Spohr, and Tobias Wunner. Interchanging Lexical Resources on the Semantic Web. *Language Resources and Evaluation*, 46(4), pages 701–719, 2012. DOI: 10.1007/s10579-012-9182-3. 19

John McCrae, Elena Montiel-Ponsoda, and Philipp Cimiano. Integrating WordNet and Wiktionary with Lemon. In Christian Chiarcos, Sebastian Nordhoff, and Sebastian Hellmann, Eds., *Linked Data in Linguistics. Representing and Connecting Language Data and Language Metadata*, pages 25–34, Springer, Berlin/Heidelberg, 2012. 19

Clifton J. McFate and Kenneth D. Forbus. NULEX: An Open-License Broad Coverage Lexicon. In *Proc. of the 48th Annual Meeting of the Association for Computational Linguistics (ACL)*, pages 363–367, Uppsala, Sweden, 2011. 22

Olena Medelyan, Catherine Legg, David Milne, and Ian H. Witten. Mining Meaning from Wikipedia. *International Journal of Human-Computer Studies*, 67(9), pages 716–754, 2009. DOI: 10.1016/j.ijhcs.2009.05.004. xvii, 12, 67

Christian M. Meyer. *Wiktionary: The Metalexicographic and the Natural Language Processing Perspective*. Ph.D. thesis, Technische Universität Darmstadt, http://tuprints.ulb.tu-darmstadt.de/3654/, 2013. 13, 14, 15, 30, 69

Christian M. Meyer and Iryna Gurevych. Worth its Weight in Gold or yet Another Resource? A Comparative Study of Wiktionary, OpenThesaurus and GermaNet. In *Computational Linguistics and Intelligent Text Processing (CICLing), 11th International Conference*, Iasi, Romania, vol. 6008 of *Lecture Notes in Computer Science*, pages 38–49, Springer, Berlin/Heidelberg, 2010. DOI: 10.1007/978-3-642-12116-6_4. 13, 23

Christian M. Meyer and Iryna Gurevych. What Psycholinguists Know about Chemistry: Aligning Wiktionary and WordNet for Increased Domain Coverage. In *Proc. of the 5th International Joint Conference on Natural Language Processing*, pages 883–892, Chiang Mai, Thailand, 2011. 35, 36, 67

Christian M. Meyer and Iryna Gurevych. OntoWiktionary: Constructing an Ontology from the Collaborative Online Dictionary Wiktionary. In Maria Teresa Pazienza and Armando Stellato,

Eds., *Semi-Automatic Ontology Development: Processes and Resources*, chapter 6, pages 131–161. IGI Global, Hershey, PA, U.S., 2012. DOI: 10.4018/978-1-4666-0188-8. 14, 68

Christian M. Meyer and Iryna Gurevych. Wiktionary: A New Rival for Expert-Built Lexicons? Exploring the Possibilities of Collaborative Lexicography. In Sylviane Granger and Magali Paquot, Eds., *Electronic Lexicography*, chapter 13, pages 259–291. Oxford University Press, 2012. DOI: 10.1093/acprof:oso/9780199654864.001.0001. 13

Rada Mihalcea. Co-Training and Self-Training for Word Sense Disambiguation. In *Proc. of the Conference on Computational Natural Language Learning (CoNLL-2004)*, pages 33–40, Boston, MA, 2004. 48

Rada Mihalcea. Using Wikipedia for Automatic Word Sense Disambiguation. In *Proc. of Human Language Technologies 2007: The Conference of the North American Chapter of the Association for Computational Linguistics (NAACL-HLT)*, pages 196–203, Rochester, NY, 2007. 22, 47

Rada Mihalcea and Ehsanul Faruque. SenseLearner: Minimally Supervised Word Sense Disambiguation for All Words in Open Text. In *Proc. of the 3rd International Workshop on the Evaluation of Systems for the Semantic Analysis of Text (SENSEVAL-3) at ACL-04*, pages 155–158, Barcelona, Spain, 2004. 47

Rada Mihalcea and Dan I. Moldovan. eXtended WordNet: Progress Report. In *Proc. of NAACL Workshop on WordNet and Other Lexical Resources*, pages 95–100, Pittsburgh, PA, 2001. 4, 38

Rada Mihalcea and Dan I. Moldovan. Automatic Generation of a Coarse Grained WordNet. In *Proc. of NAACL Workshop on WordNet and Other Lexical Resources*, pages 454–459, Pittsburgh, PA, 2001. 51

Tomas Mikolov, Ilya Sutskever, Kai Chen, Greg S Corrado, and Jeff Dean. Distributed Representations of Words and Phrases and Their Compositionality. In *Advances in Neural Information Processing Systems*, pages 3111–3119, Lake Tahoe, Nevada, 2013. 60, 64

Tristan Miller and Iryna Gurevych. WordNet-Wikipedia-Wiktionary: Construction of a Three-Way Alignment. In *Proc. of the 9th ed. of the Language Resources and Evaluation Conference*, pages 2094–2100, Reykjavik, Iceland, 2014. 23

Tristan Miller, Chris Biemann, Torsten Zesch, and Iryna Gurevych. Using Distributional Similarity for Lexical Expansion in Knowledge-Based Word Sense Disambiguation. In *Proc. of the 24th International Conference on Computational Linguistics*, pages 1781–1796, Mumbay, India, 2012. 47

David Milne and Ian H. Witten. An Effective, Low-Cost Measure of Semantic Relatedness Obtained from Wikipedia Links. In *Proc. of the AAAI Workshop on Wikipedia and Artificial Intelligence: An Evolving Synergy*, pages 25–30, Chicago, IL, 2008. 67

Mike Mintz, Steven Bills, Rion Snow, and Daniel Jurafsky. Distant Supervision for Relation Extraction without Labeled Data. In *Proc. of the Joint Conference of the 47th Annual Meeting of the Association for Computational Linguistics and the 4th International Joint Conference on Natural Language Processing*, pages 1003–1011, Singapore, 2009. DOI: 10.3115/1690219.1690287. 57

T. Mitchell, W. Cohen, E. Hruschka, P. Talukdar, J. Betteridge, A. Carlson, B. Dalvi, M. Gardner, B. Kisiel, J. Krishnamurthy, N. Lao, K. Mazaitis, T. Mohamed, N. Nakashole, E. Platanios, A. Ritter, M. Samadi, B. Settles, R. Wang, D. Wijaya, A. Gupta, X. Chen, A. Saparov, M. Greaves, and J. Welling. Never-Ending Learning. In *Proc. of the 29th AAAI Conference on Artificial Intelligence (AAAI-15)*, pages 2302–2310, Austin, TX, 2015. DOI: 10.1037/e660332010-001. 56

Marc Moens and Mark Steedman. Temporal Ontology and Temporal Reference. *Computational Linguistics*, 14(2), pages 15–28, 1988. 10

Andrea Moro, Hong Li, Sebastian Krause, Feiyu Xu, Roberto Navigli, and Hans Uszkoreit. Semantic Rule Filtering for Web-Scale Relation Extraction. In *The Semantic Web—ISWC 2013—12th International Semantic Web Conference*, Springer, Berlin/Heidelberg, 2013. DOI: 10.1007/978-3-642-41335-3_22. 59

Andrea Moro, Roberto Navigli, Francesco Maria Tucci, and Rebecca J. Passonneau. Annotating the MASC Corpus with BabelNet. In *Proc. of the 9th ed. of the Language Resources and Evaluation Conference*, pages 4214–4219, Reykjavik, Iceland, 2014. 53

Andrea Moro, Alessandro Raganato, and Roberto Navigli. Entity Linking Meets Word Sense Disambiguation: A Unified Approach. *Transactions of the Association for Computational Linguistics (TACL)*, 2, pages 231–244, 2014. 24, 49, 77

Karlheinz Mörth, Thierry Declerck, Piroska Lendvai, and Tamás Váradi. Accessing Multilingual Data on the Web for the Semantic Annotation of Cultural Heritage Texts. In *Proc. of the 2nd International Workshop on the Multilingual Semantic Web*, pages 80–85, Bonn, Germany, 2011. 69

Christof Müller and Iryna Gurevych. Using Wikipedia and Wiktionary in Domain-Specific Information Retrieval. In *Evaluating Systems for Multilingual and Multimodal Information Access—9th Workshop of the Cross-Language Evaluation Forum*, Aarhus, Denmark, 2008, vol. 5706 of *Lecture Notes in Computer Science*, pages 219–226, Springer, Berlin/Heidelberg, 2009. DOI: 10.1007/978-3-642-04447-2_28. 70, 87

Srini Narayanan, Collin Baker, Charles Fillmore, and Miriam Petruck. FrameNet Meets the Semantic Web: Lexical Semantics for the Web. In Dieter Fensel, Katia Sycara, and John Mylopoulos, Eds., *The Semantic Web—ISWC 2003*, vol. 2870 of *Lecture Notes in Computer Science*, pages 771–787, Springer, Berlin/Heidelberg, 2003. DOI: 10.1007/b14287. 19

Vivi Nastase, Michael Strube, Benjamin Boerschinger, Cäcilia Zirn, and Anas Elghafari. WikiNet: A Very Large Scale Multi-Lingual Concept Network. In *Proc. of the 7th International Conference on Language Resources and Evaluation (LREC)*, pages 1015–1022, La Valetta, Malta, 2010. 12

Roberto Navigli. Meaningful Clustering of Senses Helps Boost Word Sense Disambiguation Performance. In *Proc. of the 21st International Conference on Computational Linguistics and 44th Annual Meeting of the Association for Computational Linguistics*, pages 105–112, Sydney, Australia, 2006. DOI: 10.3115/1220175.1220189. xix, 22, 52

Roberto Navigli. Using Cycles and Quasi-Cycles to Disambiguate Dictionary Glosses. In *Proc. of the 12th Conference of the European Chapter of the Association for Computational Linguistics (EACL)*, pages 594–602, Athens, Greece, 2009. DOI: 10.3115/1609067.1609133. 39

Roberto Navigli. Word Sense Disambiguation: A Survey. *ACM Computing Surveys*, 41(2), pages 10:1–10:69, 2009. DOI: 10.1145/1459352.1459355. 46

Roberto Navigli and Simone Paolo Ponzetto. BabelNet: The Automatic Construction, Evaluation and Application of a Wide-Coverage Multilingual Semantic Network. *Artificial Intelligence*, 193, pages 217–250, 2012. DOI: 10.1016/j.artint.2012.07.001. xviii, 23, 41, 70

Roberto Navigli and Simone Paolo Ponzetto. Joining Forces Pays Off: Multilingual Joint Word Sense Disambiguation. In *Proc. of the 2012 Conference on Empirical Methods in Natural Language Processing and Natural Language Learning*, pages 1399–1410, Jeju Island, Korea, 2012. 49, 70

Roberto Navigli and Simone Paolo Ponzetto. BabelRelate! A Joint Multilingual Approach to Computing Semantic Relatedness. In *Proc. of the 26th Conference on the Advancement of Artificial Intelligence (AAAI)*, pages 108–114, Toronto, Canada, 2012. 24, 37, 68, 77

Roberto Navigli and Simone Paolo Ponzetto. Multilingual WSD with Just a Few Lines of Code: The BabelNet API. In *Proc. of the 50th Annual Meeting of the Association for Computational Linguistics (ACL)*, pages 67–72, Jeju Island, Korea, 2012. 49, 82

Roberto Navigli and Simone Paolo Ponzetto. BabelNetXplorer: A Platform for Multilingual Lexical Knowledge Base Access and Exploration. In *Proc. of the 21st World Wide Web Conference (WWW)*, pages 393–396, Lyon, France, 2012. DOI: 10.1145/2187980.2188057. 76

Roberto Navigli and Paola Velardi. Structural Semantic Interconnections: A Knowledge-Based Approach to Word Sense Disambiguation. *Pattern Analysis and Machine Intelligence, IEEE Transactions on*, 27(7), pages 1075–1086, 2005. DOI: 10.1109/tpami.2005.149. 47

Roberto Navigli, David Jürgens, and Daniele Vannella. SemEval-2013 Task 12: Multilingual Word Sense Disambiguation. In *Proc. of the 7th International Workshop on Semantic Evaluation (SemEval 2013), in conjunction with the 2nd Joint Conference on Lexical and Computational Semantics (*SEM 2013)*, pages 222–231, Atlanta, GA, 2013. 53

Arvind Neelakantan, Benjamin Roth, and Andrew McCallum. Compositional Vector Space Models for Knowledge Base Completion. In *Proc. of the 53rd Annual Meeting of the Association for Computational Linguistics and the 7th International Joint Conference on Natural Language Processing*, pages 156–166, Beijing, China, 2015. DOI: 10.3115/v1/p15-1016. 62

Elisabeth Niemann and Iryna Gurevych. The People's Web Meets Linguistic Knowledge: Automatic Sense Alignment of Wikipedia and WordNet. In *Proc. of the 9th International Conference on Computational Semantics*, pages 205–214, Oxford, UK, 2011. 35, 41

Ian Niles and Adam Pease. Towards a Standard Upper Ontology. In *Proc. of the International Conference on Formal Ontology in Information Systems*, vol. 2001, pages 2–9, Ogunquit, ME, 2001. DOI: 10.1145/505168.505170. 22

Kyoko Ohara. Semantic Annotations in Japanese FrameNet: Comparing Frames in Japanese and English. In *Proc. of the 8th International Conference on Language Resources and Evaluation (LREC 2012)*, pages 1559–1562, Istanbul, Turkey, 2012. 7

Arantxa Otegi, Xabier Arregi, Olatz Ansa, and Eneko Agirre. Using Knowledge-Based Relatedness for Information Retrieval. *Knowledge and Information Systems*, pages 1–30, 2014. DOI: 10.1007/s10115-014-0785-4. 87

Martha Palmer. SemLink: Linking PropBank, VerbNet and FrameNet. In *Proc. of the Generative Lexicon Conference*, pages 9–15, Pisa, Italy, 2009. xviii, 27, 53

Martha Palmer, Olga Babko-Malaya, and Hoa Trang Dang. Different Sense Granularities for Different Applications. In *Proc. of the 2nd Workshop on Scalable Natural Language Understanding*, pages 49–56, Boston, MA, 2004. 51

Martha Palmer, Hoa Trang Dang, and Christiane Fellbaum. Making Fine-Grained and Coarse-Grained Sense Distinctions, Both Manually and Automatically. *Natural Language Engineering*, 13(2), pages 137–163, 2007. DOI: 10.1017/s135132490500402x. 51

Rebecca J. Passonneau, Collin F. Baker, Christiane Fellbaum, and Nancy Ide. The MASC Word Sense Corpus. In *Proc. of the 8th International Conference on Language Resources and Evaluation (LREC 2012)*, pages 3025–3030, Istanbul, Turkey, 2012. 53

Siddharth Patwardhan and Ted Pedersen. Using WordNet-Based Context Vectors to Estimate the Semantic Relatedness of Concepts. In *Proc. of the EACL 2006 Workshop on Making Sense of Sense: Bringing Computational Linguistics and Psycholinguistics Together*, pages 1–8, Trento, Italy, 2006. 67

Ted Pedersen. Unsupervised Corpus-Based Methods for WSD. In Eneko Agirre and Philip Edmonds, Eds., *Word Sense Disambiguation: Algorithms and Applications*, vol. 33 of *Text, Speech and Language Technology*, pages 133–166, Springer, 2006. DOI: 10.1007/978-1-4020-4809-8. 48

Ted Pedersen, Satanjeev Banerjee, and Siddharth Patwardhan. Maximizing Semantic Relatedness to Perform Word Sense Disambiguation. *University of Minnesota Supercomputing Institute Research Report UMSI*, 25, 2005. 47

Jeffrey Pennington, Richard Socher, and Christopher D. Manning. GloVe: Global Vectors for Word Representation. In *Proc. of the 2014 Conference on Empirical Methods in Natural Language Processing*, pages 1532–1543, Doha, Qatar, 2014. DOI: 10.3115/v1/d14-1162. 60

Wim Peters, Ivonne Peters, and Piek Vossen. Automatic Sense Clustering in EuroWordNet. In *Proc. of the 1st International Conference on Language Resources and Evaluation*, pages 409–416, Granada, Spain, 1998. 51

Emanuele Pianta, Luisa Bentivogli, and Christian Girardi. MultiWordNet: Developing an Aligned Multilingual Database. In *Proc. of the 1st International Global WordNet Conference*, pages 293–302, Mysore, India, 2002. 26, 69

Mohammad Taher Pilehvar and Roberto Navigli. A Robust Approach to Aligning Heterogeneous Lexical Resources. In *Proc. of the 52nd Conference of the Association for Computational Linguistics*, pages 468–475, Baltimore, MD, 2014. DOI: 10.3115/v1/p14-1044. 35, 42, 87

Mohammad Taher Pilehvar, David Jürgens, and Roberto Navigli. Align, Disambiguate and Walk: A Unified Approach for Measuring Semantic Similarity. In *Proc. of the 51st Conference of the Association for Computational Linguistics*, pages 1341–1351, Sofia, Bulgaria, 2013. 67

Massimo Poesio, Jon Chamberlain, Udo Kruschwitz, Livio Robaldo, and Luca Ducceschi. Phrase Detectives: Utilizing Collective Intelligence for Internet-Scale Language Resource Creation. *ACM Transactions on Interactive Intelligent Systems*, 3(1), pages 3:1–3:44, 2013. DOI: 10.1145/2448116.2448119. 80

Simone Paolo Ponzetto and Roberto Navigli. Large-Scale Taxonomy Mapping for Restructuring and Integrating Wikipedia. In *Proc. of the 21th International Joint Conference on Artificial Intelligence (IJCAI)*, pages 2083–2088, Pasadena, CA, 2009. 38, 41

Simone Paolo Ponzetto and Roberto Navigli. Knowledge-Rich Word Sense Disambiguation Rivaling Supervised Systems. In *Proc. of the 48th Annual Meeting of the Association for Computational Linguistics (ACL)*, pages 1522–1531, Uppsala, Sweden, 2010. 48

Martin Potthast, Benno Stein, and Maik Anderka. A Wikipedia-Based Multilingual Retrieval Model. *Lecture Notes in Computer Science*, vol. 4956, pages 522–530, Springer, Berlin/Heidelberg, 2008. DOI: 10.1007/978-3-540-78646-7_51. 70

Quentin Pradet, Laurence Danlos, and Gaël De Chalendar. Adapting VerbNet to French Using Existing Resources. In *Proc. of the 9th ed. of the Language Resources and Evaluation Conference*, pages 1122–1126, Reykjavik, Iceland, 2014. 10

Sameer S. Pradhan, Edward Loper, Dmitriy Dligach, and Martha Palmer. SemEval-2007, Task-17: English Lexical Sample, SRL and All Words. In *Proc. of SemEval-2007*, pages 87–92, Prague, Czech Republic, 2007. DOI: 10.3115/1621474.1621490. 52, 53

Roy Rada, Hafedh Mili, Ellen Bicknell, and Maria Blettner. Development and Application of a Metric on Semantic Nets. *IEEE Transactions on Systems, Man and Cybernetics*, 19(1), pages 17–30, 1989. DOI: 10.1109/21.24528. 37

Stephen L. Reed and Douglas B. Lenat. Mapping Ontologies into Cyc. In *Proc. of the AAAI Workshop on Ontologies and the Semantic Web*, pages 1–6, Edmonton, Canada, 2002. 22, 27

Philip Resnik and David Yarowsky. Distinguishing Systems and Distinguishing Senses: New Evaluation Methods for Word Sense Disambiguation. *Natural Language Engineering*, 5(3), pages 113–133, 2000. DOI: 10.1017/s1351324999002211. 51

Sebastian Riedel, Limin Yao, and Andrew McCallum. Modeling Relations and Their Mentions without Labeled Text. In José Luis Balcàzar, Francesco Bonchi, Aristides Gionis, and Michèle Sebag, Eds., *Machine Learning and Knowledge Discovery in Databases*, vol. 6323 of *Lecture Notes in Computer Science*, pages 148–163, Springer, Berlin/Heidelberg, 2010. DOI: 10.1007/978-3-642-15939-8. 58, 59

Sebastian Riedel, Limin Yao, Andrew McCallum, and Benjamin M. Marlin. Relation Extraction with Matrix Factorization and Universal Schemas. In *Proc. of the Human Language Technology Conference of the North American Chapter of the Association for Computational Linguistics*, pages 74–84, Atlanta, GA, 2013. 62

Sascha Rothe and Hinrich Schütze. AutoExtend: Extending Word Embeddings to Embeddings for Synsets and Lexemes. In *Proc. of the 53rd Annual Meeting of the Association for Computational Linguistics and the 7th International Joint Conference on Natural Language Processing*, pages 1793–1803, Beijing, China, 2015. DOI: 10.3115/v1/p15-1173. 64

Maria Ruiz-Casado, Enrique Alfonseca, and Pablo Castells. Automatic Assignment of Wikipedia Encyclopedic Entries to WordNet Synsets. In *Advances in Web Intelligence: Proc. of the 3rd International Atlantic Web Intelligence Conference*, Lodz, Poland, 2005, vol. 3528 of *Lecture Notes in Computer Science*, pages 380–386, Springer, Berlin/Heidelberg, 2005. DOI: 10.1007/11495772_59. 25

Josef Ruppenhofer, Michael Ellsworth, Miriam R. L. Petruck, Christopher R. Johnson, and Jan Scheffczyk. FrameNet II: Extended Theory and Practice. *International Computer Science Institute*, Berkeley, CA, 2010. xviii, 6

Jacek Rzeniewicz and Julian Szymański. Bringing Common Sense to WordNet with a Word Game. In Costin Badica, Ngoc Thanh Nguyen, and Marius Brezovan, Eds., *Computational Collective Intelligence. Technologies and Applications—5th International Conference, ICCCI 2013*, Craiova, Romania, vol. 8083 of *Lecture Notes in Computer Science*, pages 296–305, Springer Berlin/Heidelberg, 2013. DOI: 10.1007/978-3-642-40495-5. 80

Cristina Sarasua, Elena Simperl, and Natalya F. Noy. CrowdMap: Crowdsourcing Ontology Alignment with Microtasks. In *Proc. of the 11th International Conference on The Semantic Web*, Boston, MA, pages 525–541, Springer-Verlag, Berlin/Heidelberg, 2012. DOI: 10.1007/978-3-642-35176-1_33. 80

Carolina Scarton and Sandra Aluísio. Towards a Cross-Linguistic VerbNet-Style Lexicon for Brazilian Portuguese. In *Proc. of the LREC 2012 Workshop on Creating Cross-Language Resources for Disconnected Languages and Styles*, pages 11–18, Istanbul, Turkey, 2012. 10

Uwe Schöning. Graph Isomorphism is in the Low Hierarchy. *Journal of Computer and System Sciences*, 37(3), pages 312–323, 1988. DOI: 10.1016/0022-0000(88)90010-4. 32

Nitin Seemakurty, Jonathan Chu, Luis von Ahn, and Anthony Tomasic. Word Sense Disambiguation via Human Computation. In *Proc. of the ACM SIGKDD Workshop on Human Computation*, Washington DC, pages 60–63, New York, 2010. DOI: 10.1145/1837885.1837905. 80

Gilles Sérasset. DBnary: Wiktionary as a lemon-Based RDF Multilingual Lexical Resource. *Semantic Web*, 6(4), pages 355–361, 2015. DOI: 10.3233/sw-140147. 14, 19

Gilles Sérasset and Andon Tchechmedjiev. Wiktionary as Linked Data for 12 Language Editions with Enhanced Translation Relations. In *3rd Workshop on Linked Data in Linguistics: Multilingual Knowledge Resources and Natural Language Processing, collocated with the 9th ed. of the Language Resources and Evaluation Conference*, pages 68–71 Reykjavik, Iceland, 2014. 13

Lei Shi and Rada Mihalcea. Putting Pieces Together: Combining FrameNet, VerbNet and WordNet for Robust Semantic Parsing. In *Computational Linguistics and Intelligent Text Processing (CICLing), 6th International Conference*, Mexico City, 2005, vol. 3406 of *Lecture Notes in Computer Science*, pages 100–111, 2005. DOI: 10.1007/978-3-540-30586-6_9. xviii, 22, 48

Vered Shwartz, Omer Levy, Ido Dagan, and Jacob Goldberger. Learning to Exploit Structure Resources for Lexical Inference. In *Proc. of Nineteenth Conference on Computational Natural Language Learning (CoNLL)*, pages 175–184, Beijing, China, 2015. xiii

Jakub Simko, Michal Tvarozek, and Maria Bielikova. Little Search Game: Term Network Acquisition via a Human Computation Game. In *Proc. of the 22nd ACM Conference on Hypertext and Hypermedia*, pages 57–62, Eindhoven, The Netherlands, New York, 2011. 80 DOI: 10.1145/1995966.1995977.

Katharina Siorpaes and Martin Hepp. Games with a Purpose for the Semantic Web. *IEEE Intelligent Systems*, 23(3), pages 50–60, 2008. DOI: 10.1109/mis.2008.45. 80

Rion Snow, Sushant Prakash, Daniel Jurafsky, and Andrew Y. Ng. Learning to Merge Word Senses. In *Proc. of the 2007 Joint Conference on Empirical Methods in Natural Language Processing and Computational Language Learning*, pages 1005–1014, Prague, Czech Republic, 2007. 51, 52

Benjamin Snyder and Martha Palmer. The English All-Words Task. In *Proc. of the 3rd International Workshop on the Evaluation of Systems for the Semantic Analysis of Text (SENSEVAL-3) at ACL-04*, pages 41–43, Barcelona, Spain, 2004. 53

Catherine Soanes and Angus Stevenson, Eds. *Oxford Dictionary of English*. Oxford University Press, Oxford, 2003. 3, 52

Richard Socher, Danqi Chen, Christopher D. Manning, and Andrew Y. Ng. Reasoning with Neural Tensor Networks for Knowledge Base Completion. In *Advances in Neural Information Processing Systems 26*, pages 926–934, 2013. 62

Harold Somers. Translation Memory Systems. In Harold Somers, Ed., *Computers and Translation: A Translator's Guide*, vol. 35 of *Benjamins Translation Library*, chapter 3, pages 31–47, John Benjamins Publishing, Amsterdam, 2003. DOI: 10.1075/btl.35. 68

Claudia Soria, Monica Monachini, and Piek Vossen. WordNet-LMF: Fleshing out a Standardized Format for WordNet Interoperability. In *Proc. of the International Workshop on Intercultural Collaboration*, pages 139–146, Palo Alto, CA, 2009. DOI: 10.1145/1499224.1499246. 18

Dennis Spohr, Philipp Cimiano, and Laura Hollink. Multilingual and Cross-Lingual Ontology Matching and its Application to Financial Accounting Standards. In *Proc. of the 10th International Semantic Web Conference (ISWC 2011)*, pages 665–680, Bonn, Germany, 2011. 36

Sofia Stamou, Kemal Oflazer, Karel Pala, Dimitris Christoudoulakis, Dan Cristea, Dan Tufi, Svetla Koeva, Gheorghi Totkov, Dominique Dutoit, and Maria Grigoriadou. BalkaNet: A Multilingual Semantic Network for the Balkan Languages. In *Proc. of the 1st International Global WordNet Conference*, pages 12–14, Mysore, India, 2002. 26, 69

Pontus Stenetorp, Sampo Pyysalo, Goran Topić, Tomoko Ohta, Sophia Ananiadou, and Jun'ichi Tsujii. BRAT: A Web-Based Tool for NLP-Assisted Text Annotation. In *Proc. of the 13th Conference of the European Chapter of the Association for Computational Linguistics (EACL)*, pages 102–107, Avignon, France, 2012. 80

Carlos Subirats and Hiroaki Sato. Spanish FrameNet and FrameSQL. In *Proc. of the Workshop on Building Lexical Resources from Semantically Annotated Corpora collocated with the 4th International Conference on Language Resources and Evaluation*, pages 13–16, Lisbon, Portugal, 2004. 7

Fabian M. Suchanek, Gjergji Kasneci, and Gerhard Weikum. YAGO: A Core of Semantic Knowledge. In *Proc. of the 16th World Wide Web Conference (WWW)*, pages 697–706, Banff, Canada, 2007. DOI: 10.1145/1242572.1242667. 12, 25

Fabian M. Suchanek, Gjergji Kasneci, and Gerhard Weikum. YAGO: A Large Ontology from Wikipedia and WordNet. *Web Semantics*, 6(3), pages 203–217, 2008. DOI: 10.1016/j.websem.2008.06.001. 25

Sebastian Sulger, Miriam Butt, Tracy Holloway King, Paul Meurer, Tibor Laczkó, György Rákosi, Cheikh Bamba Dione, Helge Dyvik, Victoria Rosén, Koenraad De Smedt, Agnieszka Patejuk, Ozlem Cetinoglu, I Wayan Arka, and Meladel Mistica. ParGramBank: The ParGram Parallel Treebank. In *Proc. of the 51st Conference of the Association for Computational Linguistics*, pages 550–560, Sofia, Bulgaria, 2013. 7

Mihai Surdeanu, Julie Tibshirani, Ramesh Nallapati, and Christopher D. Manning. Multi-Instance Multi-Label Learning for Relation Extraction. In *Proc. of the 2012 Conference on Empirical Methods in Natural Language Processing and Natural Language Learning*, pages 455–465, Jeju Island, Korea, 2012. 59

James Surowiecki. *The Wisdom of Crowds*. Anchor Books, New York, 2005. DOI: 10.1119/1.2423042. xvii, 11, 69

Takenobu Tokunaga, Dain Kaplan, Nicoletta Calzolari, Monica Monachini, Claudia Soria, Virach Sornlertlamvanich, Thatsanee Charoenporn, Yingju Xia, Chu-Ren Huang, Shu-Kai Hsieh, and Kiyoaki Shirai. Query Expansion Using LMF-Compliant Lexical Resources. In *Proc. of the 7th Workshop on Asian Language Resources*, pages 145–152, Suntec, Singapore, 2009. DOI: 10.3115/1690299.1690320. 16

Noriko Tomuro. Tree-Cut and a Lexicon Based on Systematic Polysemy. In *Proc. of the 2nd Conference of the North American Chapter of the Association for Computational Linguistics*, pages 1010–1017, Pittsburgh, PA, 2001. DOI: 10.3115/1073336.1073346. 51

Sara Tonelli and Daniele Pighin. New Features for FrameNet—WordNet Mapping. In *Proc. of the 13th Conference on Computational Natural Language Learning (CoNLL)*, pages 219–227, Boulder, Colorado, Association for Computational Linguistics, 2009. DOI: 10.3115/1596374.1596408. 26

Antonio Toral, Rafael Muñoz, and Monica Monachini. Named Entity WordNet. In *Proc. of the 6th International Conference on Language Resources and Evaluation (LREC)*, pages 741–747, Marrakech, Morocco, 2008. 38

Antonio Toral, Oscar Ferrandez, Eneko Agirre, and Rafael Munoz. A Study on Linking Wikipedia Categories to WordNet Synsets Using Text Similarity. In *Proc. of the International Conference on Recent Advances in Natural Language Processing*, pages 449–454, Borovets, Bulgaria, 2009.

Antonio Toral, Stefania Bracale, Monica Monachini, and Claudia Soria. Rejuvenating the Italian WordNet: Upgrading, Standarising, Extending. In *Proc. of the 5th International Global WordNet Conference*, Mumbai, India, 2010. 5, 18

Antonio Toral, Monica Monachini, Claudia Soria, Montse Cuadros, German Rigau, Wauter Bosma, and Piek Vossen. Linking a Domain Thesaurus to WordNet and Conversion to WordNet-LMF. In *Proc. of the 5th Joint ISO-ACL/SIGSEM Workshop on Interoperable Semantic Annotation*, Hong Kong, 2010. 25

Kristina Toutanova, Danqi Chen, Patrick Pantel, Hoifung Poon, Pallavi Choudhury, and Michael Gamon. Representing Text for Joint Embedding of Text and Knowledge Bases. In *Proc. of the 2015 Conference on Empirical Methods in Natural Language Processing*, pages 1499–1509, Lisbon, Portugal, 2015. DOI: 10.18653/v1/d15-1174. 62

Mark Van Assem, Aldo Gangemi, and Guus Schreiber. Conversion of WordNet to a Standard RDF/OWL Representation. In *Proc. of the 5th International Conference on Language Resources and Evaluation*, pages 237–242, Genoa, Italy, 2006. 19

Daniele Vannella, David Jürgens, Daniele Scarfini, Domenico Toscani, and Roberto Navigli. Validating and Extending Semantic Knowledge Bases Using Video Games with a Purpose. In *Proc. of the 52nd Conference of the Association for Computational Linguistics*, pages 1294–1304, Baltimore, MD, 2014. DOI: 10.3115/v1/p14-1122. 80

Tony Veale, Nuno Seco, and Jer Hayes. Creative Discovery in Lexical Ontologies. In *Proc. of the 20th International Conference on Computational Linguistics*, pages 1333–1338, Geneva, Switzerland, 2004. DOI: 10.3115/1220355.1220550. 29

Noortje J. Venhuizen, Valerio Basile, Kilian Evang, and Johan Bos. Gamification for Word Sense Labeling. In *Proc. of the 10th International Conference on Computational Semantics (IWCS 2013)*, pages 397–403, Potsdam, Germany, 2013. 80

Marta Villegas and Núria Bel. PAROLE/SIMPLE "lemon" Ontology and Lexicons. *Semantic Web*, 6(4), pages 363–369, 2015. DOI: 10.3233/sw-140148. 8, 19

Luis von Ahn and Laura Dabbish. Labeling Images with a Computer Game. In *Proc. of the SIGCHI Conference on Human Factors in Computing Systems (CHI '04)*, pages 319–326, Vienna, Austria, 2004. DOI: 10.1145/985692.985733. 80

Piek Vossen, Ed. *EuroWordNet: A Multilingual Database with Lexical Semantic Networks*. Kluwer Academic Publishers, 1998. DOI: 10.1007/978-94-017-1491-4. 26, 69

Piek Vossen, Claudia Soria, and Monica Monachini. Wordnet-LMF: A Standard Representation for Multilingual Wordnets. In Gil Francopoulo, Ed., *LMF: Lexical Markup Framework*, Computer Engineering and IT, chapter 4, pages 51–66. Wiley-ISTE, London, 2013. DOI: 10.1002/9781118712696. 18

Tong Wang, Abdelrahman Mohamed, and Graeme Hirst. Learning Lexical Embeddings with Syntactic and Lexicographic Knowledge. In *Proc. of the 53rd Annual Meeting of the Association for Computational Linguistics and the 7th International Joint Conference on Natural Language Processing*, pages 458–463, Beijing, China, 2015. DOI: 10.3115/v1/p15-2075. 65

Robert West, Evgeniy Gabrilovich, Kevin Murphy, Shaohua Sun, Rahul Gupta, and Dekang Lin. Knowledge Base Completion via Search-Based Question Answering. In *Proc. of the 23rd International Conference on World Wide Web*, pages 515–526, Seoul, Korea, 2014. DOI: 10.1145/2566486.2568032. 62

Jason Weston, Antoine Bordes, Oksana Yakhnenko, and Nicolas Usunier. Connecting Language and Knowledge Bases with Embedding Models for Relation Extraction. In *Joint Conference on Empirical Methods in Natural Language Processing and Computational Natural Language Learning*, pages 1366–1371, Seattle, WA, 2013. 57, 59, 62

Menzo Windhouwer and Sue Ellen Wright. LMF and the Data Category Registry: Principles and Applications. In Gil Francopoulo, Ed., *LMF: Lexical Markup Framework*, Computer Engineering and IT, chapter 3, pages 41–50. Wiley-ISTE, London, 2013. DOI: 10.1002/9781118712696. 17

Bishan Yang, Wen-tau Yih, Xiaodong He, Jianfeng Gao, and Li Deng. Embedding Entities and Relations for Learning and Inference in Knowledge Bases. In *Proc. of the International Conference on Learning Representations (ICLR)*, San Diego, CA, 2015. 62

David Yarowsky. Unsupervised Word Sense Disambiguation Rivaling Supervised Methods. In *Proc. of the 33rd annual meeting on Association for Computational Linguistics*, pages 189–196, Cambridge, Massachusetts, 1995. DOI: 10.3115/981658.981684. 48

Mikalai Yatskevich and Fausto Giunchiglia. Element Level Semantic Matching Using WordNet. In *Meaning Coordination and Negotiation Workshop at 3rd International Semantic Web Conference (ISWC 2004)*, pages 37–48, Hiroshima, Japan, 2004. 30

Seid Muhie Yimam, Iryna Gurevych, Richard Eckart de Castilho, and Chris Biemann. Web-Anno: A Flexible, Web-Based and Visually Supported System for Distributed Annotations. In *Proc. of the 51st Conference of the Association for Computational Linguistics*, pages 1–6, Sofia, Bulgaria, 2013. 80

Mo Yu and Mark Dredze. Improving Lexical Embeddings with Semantic Knowledge. In *Proc. of the 52nd Conference of the Association for Computational Linguistics*, pages 545–550, Baltimore, MD, 2014. DOI: 10.3115/v1/p14-2089. 64

Deniz Yuret. Some Experiments with a Naive Bayes WSD System. In *Proc. of the 3rd International Workshop on the Evaluation of Systems for the Semantic Analysis of Text (SENSEVAL-3) at ACL-04*, pages 265–268, Barcelona, Spain, 2004. 48

Annie Zaenen, Lauri Karttunen, and Richard Crouch. Local Textual Inference: Can it be Defined or Circumscribed? In *Proc. of the ACL Workshop on Empirical Modeling of Semantic Equivalence and Entailment*, pages 31–36, Ann Arbor, MI, 2005. DOI: 10.3115/1631862.1631868. 67

Torsten Zesch and Iryna Gurevych. Wisdom of Crowds Versus Wisdom of Linguists—Measuring the Semantic Relatedness of Words. *Journal of Natural Language Engineering*, 16(01), pages 25–59, 2010. DOI: 10.1017/s1351324909990167. 67

Torsten Zesch, Iryna Gurevych, and Max Mühlhäuser. Analyzing and Accessing Wikipedia as a Lexical Semantic Resource. In *Proc. of the Biennial GLDV Conference*, pages 197–205, Tübingen, Germany, 2007. 12

Torsten Zesch, Christof Müller, and Iryna Gurevych. Using Wiktionary for Computing Semantic Relatedness. In *Proc. of the 23rd Conference on the Advancement of Artificial Intelligence (AAAI)*, pages 861–867, Chicago, IL, 2008. 37, 67

Torsten Zesch, Christof Müller, and Iryna Gurevych. Extracting Lexical Semantic Knowledge from Wikipedia and Wiktionary. In *Proc. of the 6th International Conference on Language Resources and Evaluation (LREC)*, pages 1646–1652, Marrakech, Morocco, 2008. 13

Huaping Zhong, Jianwen Zhang, Zhen Wang, Hai Wan, and Zheng Chen. Aligning Knowledge and Text Embeddings by Entity Descriptions. In *Proc. of the 2015 Conference on Empirical Methods in Natural Language Processing*, pages 267–272, Lisbon, Portugal, 2015. DOI: 10.18653/v1/d15-1031. 63

Authors' Biographies

IRYNA GUREVYCH

Iryna Gurevych is Full Professor and Director of the Ubiquitous Knowledge Processing (UKP) Lab in the Department of Computer Science at the Technische Universität Darmstadt. In addition, she leads the Graduate School "Adaptive Information Preparation from Heterogeneous Sources" (AIPHES). Within NLP, Iryna's research focus is on text understanding and lexical semantics, argumentation analysis, and novel applications of text analysis in social sciences and humanities. Iryna has led the development of UBY, a large-scale sense-linked lexical-semantic resource for English and German. She has published on using this resource to enhance various natural language processing tasks, such as word sense disambiguation, text classification, or information search, and has done significant research on semantic relatedness and semantic similarity of words, short texts, or longer documents.

JUDITH ECKLE-KOHLER

Judith Eckle-Kohler is currently a postdoctoral researcher at the Ubiquitous Knowledge Processing (UKP) Lab in the Department of Computer Science at the Technische Universität Darmstadt. She obtained her doctoral degree in Computational Linguistics in 1999 from the University of Stuttgart, Germany. She also holds a Diploma in Computer Science (University of Stuttgart, 1995). Her current research interests are knowledge-based machine learning and large-scale knowledge acquisition from text. Within the UBY project, she has been leading the creation of the uniform data model UBY-LMF, and developed distant supervision methods based on UBY for the tasks of verb sense disambiguation and semantic role labeling.

MICHAEL MATUSCHEK

Michael Matuschek is currently working as a software engineer and consultant in Munich, Germany. Before that, he was a researcher at the Ubiquitous Knowledge Processing (UKP) Lab in the Department of Computer Science at the Technische Universität Darmstadt, where he also received his doctoral degree in Computer Science in 2014. The main topic of his academic research work was the automatic linking of lexical resources in the course of the UBY project, with a particular interest in collaboratively constructed ones. Nowadays his work is more focused on practical implementations of NLP, for instance in business intelligence applications and human computer interaction.